A Spiritual Blueprint *for* Humanity

ROZAK TATEBE

Translated by Alana Simpson

BALBOA.PRESS
A DIVISION OF HAY HOUSE

Balboa Press books may be ordered through booksellers or by contacting:

Balboa Press
A Division of Hay House
1663 Liberty Drive
Bloomington, IN 47403
www.balboapress.com.au
AU TFN: 1 800 844 925 (Toll Free inside Australia)
AU Local: 0283 107 086 (+61 2 8310 7086 from outside Australia)

Because of the dynamic nature of the Internet, any web addresses or links contained in
this book may have changed since publication and may no longer be valid. The views
expressed in this work are solely those of the author and do not necessarily reflect the
views of the publisher, and the publisher hereby disclaims any responsibility for them.

The author of this book does not dispense medical advice or prescribe the use
of any technique as a form of treatment for physical, emotional, or medical
problems without the advice of a physician, either directly or indirectly. The
intent of the author is only to offer information of a general nature to help you
in your quest for emotional and spiritual well-being. In the event you use any
of the information in this book for yourself, which is your constitutional right,
the author and the publisher assume no responsibility for your actions.

Any people depicted in stock imagery provided by Getty Images are
models, and such images are being used for illustrative purposes only.
Certain stock imagery © Getty Images.

Print information available on the last page.

ISBN: 978-1-5043-2466-3 (sc)
ISBN: 978-1-5043-2467-0 (e)

Balboa Press rev. date: 02/24/2021

CONTENTS

FOREWORD

In 1925, a young Indonesian was out walking one night when a brilliant ball of light descended from the sky and entered his body, a light that lit up the whole countryside and was witnessed by many others in the locality. The light initiated a strong vibration within his being, a manifestation of the Great Life Force, which, years later, he was to speak of as "This power ... is the vibration that exists within all things. It is the basis or the beginning of the whole universe."

The young man, now known around the world as Bapak, was just twenty-four years old, and when this power arose within him, his first thought was that he must be suffering a heart attack. He returned home and lay down, expecting to die. Instead, he was moved to stand up and pray, and this altered state was to arise within him every night thereafter for the next three years. Throughout this time, he hardly slept, while continuing to maintain a job and all other normal responsibilities of family and daily life.

During these years, Bapak encountered an infinite variety of inner and outer experiences as an extraordinary process of spiritual transformation and realization unfolded within him. Eight years later, after a spiritual ascension that took him "through all the heavens," he was given a "key" and guided to understand that it was his mission to transmit this inner contact to all who asked for it.

So began the spread of the movement that came to be known as Subud, an acronym for *Susila, Budhi, Dharma,* which can be summarized to mean "right living from within according to the will of God." In due course, the very same contact with the Great Life Force that Bapak himself had first received spread to more than eighty countries, and in 1954, Rozak Tatebe was among the first to receive it outside Indonesia. In addition to steeping himself in the wisdom and guidance to which Bapak gave voice during his lifetime, the author went on to spend time with him, both in Japan and in Indonesia. Now aged ninety-two, he is therefore uniquely placed to offer this elucidation of what Bapak channeled to humankind and of its significance for the future of the human race.

Bapak himself described the Latihan as the spiritual reality that lies at the heart of all the great religions: the inner truth for which seekers in every age have yearned. He often reminded people that the Latihan is a gift beyond price, a timely intervention from On High that has come about in our era because the increasingly powerful influence of the material life force now seriously threatens the peace and very survival of the world.

The author takes something of an erudite look at the development of science over the centuries, recognizing that the notion of God and the soul still has not fully recovered from the prosecution of Galileo in the seventeenth century. He sees this ongoing conflict between science and religion as being epitomized in the life of the French medical scientist Alexis Carrel (1873–1944). Carrel won the Nobel Prize in Physiology or Medicine, but his scientific worldview was severely challenged when he witnessed the miraculous healing at the Marian Shrine at Lourdes of a patient he had believed would die within days.

But need there be such a conflict? Could there not instead be a partnership, a collaboration between the mind and the inner spiritual reality of the true human being? While in no way denigrating the mind and its role in our lives and in the growth of science, Rozak Tatebe explains how the Latihan of Subud brings to life the often-dormant inner self and works to reestablish its rightful relationship both with the Creator and with His creation. With the true self in the driving seat, the human being is no longer at the mercy of greed, anger, and self-interest, which in turn threaten the very peace of the world.

Enriched by accounts of his own experiences, Rozak covers a great deal of ground in this absorbing read, looking at the afterlife, the nature of beings on other planets, and so much more. Above all, he reveals how Bapak's new cosmology constitutes a grand design for the future of the human race.

—Emmanuel Elliott, author of *The Dawning*

INTRODUCTION

The Three Questions

Paul Gauguin, a leading French painter of the nineteenth century, inscribed three questions on a painting he regarded as one of his masterpieces. The painting is simply titled *Where Do We Come From?* and the three enduring questions he asked are:

Where did we come from?

What are we?

Where are we going?

Gauguin was disillusioned with the inhumanity of modern civilization and urban culture, and he later moved to Tahiti in search of a primitive society. However, there too, he witnessed the ravage of Tahiti by modern civilization and, despairing, vowed to commit suicide. Fortunately, he failed in this attempt, and the *Where Do We Come From?* painting that he executed around the same time is preserved at the Boston Museum of Art. The three questions he poses in this painting continue to be unanswered more than one hundred years later.

Now the world is in a state of rapid transformation. The revolution in data and communications technology has brought the world together, and this wave of civilization has reached around the globe, with no society left untouched. While civilization brought us many benefits, communities everywhere are being distorted in ways we can no longer ignore.

Today, human beings are surrounded by human-made structures rather than living with or within nature. It is little wonder that we, who are born from nature, are more and more subject to invisible stresses. These manifest as physical anomalies such as allergies, near-sightedness, or depression. Even the way we think is being altered. As we absorb more and more materialism, our minds become increasingly materialistic and dehumanized, and we start to objectify those around us. Instead of using science, the champion of modern civilization, to uncover our ultimate destination as a race, most people seem indifferent to this question, nor is it considered an orthodox subject of study.

This book aims to shed a new light on the eternal mystery of humanity, so dramatically depicted by Gauguin, as well as suggesting a blueprint for our shared future. To find this light, I looked to the new understanding of the human mind, the reality of life, and the spiritual universe, which was brought to the world by Pak Muhammad Subuh, the founder of the Subud movement.

To start, let us look at how much we already know and understand about ourselves and the world in line with the facts we have uncovered so far.

CHAPTER 1

THE HISTORY OF EARTH AND LIFE

The Birth of the Universe and Earth

Our earth is just one of the planets that orbit the sun. Science tells us that the big bang was the starting point of the universe about 13.7 billion years ago, and the Milky Way galaxy, which includes the sun and the earth, was created about 4.5 billion years ago. The most prevalent theory for the origin of life states that the newly created earth was a hot fireball that gradually cooled, and 700 million years later, life first appeared on the planet. This was around 3.8 billion years ago. Evidence of this process is traceable in layers of soil and fossils.

This time span was quite short if we consider the many conditions that need to be met for life to form in planets like Earth. The first condition is the presence of water: living organisms cannot exist without water, as water makes up most of their composition. Seventy percent of the earth's surface is water in the form of huge oceans and seas and other bodies of water.

Then there is the vital issue of distance from the biggest source of light and heat, the sun. Life cannot emerge if the temperature is too hot or too cold.

Next, the planet must be enclosed in an atmosphere that includes oxygen, carbon dioxide, and nitrogen. Oxygen is essential for life, as organisms use this to access nutrients to create heat and energy in the body. There must be oxygen in the water for fish to survive. Carbon dioxide is essential for plants; without it, they cannot convert sunlight into nutritional energy through photosynthesis, nor can they supply life-giving oxygen to other organisms. Nitrogen is also vital for all organisms and another fertilizing element for plants.

The cosmos is equally complex and is subject to the same natural constants as Earth, such as gravitational and electromagnetic wave constants. These constants were most likely determined during the big bang and the birth of the universe. If, for some reason, even one of those constants had differed slightly, the universe would never have been born, the sun and the earth would not have existed, and we ourselves would not exist. These natural constants are all within a range that fully supports human survival and the existence of the sun and the earth. Humans were born on Earth with the universe within our gaze.

These facts are both impossible and miraculous. Even with complex mathematical calculations, the probability of such a perfect match of these natural constants occurring simultaneously in nature is close to zero. Why did this impossible situation arise? This is the mystery and the first question we ask of the universe and the earth.

The Human Principle and the Multiverse Theory

The challenges posed by this mystery continue to be tackled by science, and the responses can be roughly summarized into the following two categories.

The first is the idea that this improbable event occurred through the involvement of a superhuman intelligence in the creation of the universe. This theory is called the human principle.

The second theory is the multiverse idea, which posits that this seemingly impossible event occurred not because of some superintelligence but because many universes exist simultaneously. It is impossible to calculate the probability of the alignment of these events if only one universe exists. However, if there is an infinite number of universes, it is not improbable that these extraordinary conditions could exist in one of them. The belief is that the universe emerged with the big bang not from an empty vacuum but from a "vacuum" that contained energy. In that explosion, elementary particles were born that then started to form universes, and each one of those elementary particles created their own separate universe at that time.

The human principle theory admits the existence of a superintelligence that is beyond humankind—but not necessarily attributable to God—and debates whether this is related to the creation of the universe. The scientific community still appears to have an objection to using the word *God*. Modern science was born in the fire of a conflict between science and religion in seventeenth-century Europe, symbolized by the famous court trial of Galileo Galilei. In this trial, Galileo argued the Copernican theory, which claims that the earth and stars revolve around the sun, as opposed to the Bible-based Ptolemaic theory of the Christian theologians, which states that the earth is the center of the universe and the sun and stars are immovably affixed to the earth's sky.

The theologians won the court case, but Galileo is reported to have murmured at the time, "E pur, si muove" (Even so, it does move). Later, scientific findings that supported Galileo's theory came thick and fast, until finally science prevailed and his thinking was vindicated. However, this traumatic conflict had a lasting impact on science, and the idea that God and religion are enemies of science and should be denied existence was, and continues to be, widely accepted in the scientific community.

Science was originally a division of philosophy that the ancient Greeks called *natural science*. In the Christianity-dominated Middle Ages, science was viewed as a servant to theology. However, as a result of the Galileo controversy, science gradually became independent, new methodologies were established, and modern science was born.

To clearly separate science from religion and philosophy, these new methodologies used mathematical algorithms alongside observation and experimentation. Scientists started quantifying their research subjects and expressing the resulting data in mathematical formulas so that they could draw correct conclusions. Galileo once said that the book of nature is written in the language of geometry. The laws of nature are expressed in mathematical formulas, and the relationship between these laws is best explained through mathematical theorems. For that reason, mathematics can be considered as a more appropriate language for science than natural language.

However, while these new methodologies expanded the objectivity and logicality of science, they also greatly narrowed the scope of science, because anything that could not be quantified or expressed as a mathematical formula could not be included as a subject for study. For that reason, God, the soul, and the world after death were excluded as subjects of science and ignored. If science could not confirm the existence of something, that *something* was falsely believed to not exist in the first place. This ruled out the study of spiritual subjects and even the study of the human mind: How could the mind itself be quantified?

While psychology is generally considered to be the study of the mind, current psychology does not study the mind so much as human behavior. Psychology observes and quantifies behavior and infers the feelings that motivate that behavior. Since it is a science, psychology can only study behaviors that can be categorized and quantified. Some people are aware that science is constrained by shortcomings such as these, but for the most part, society does not recognize this. Most people still trust scientific knowledge unconditionally, and their lives revolve around this trust. The miraculous fact that all the earth's natural constants were within the range required to give birth to all living things continues to puzzle scientists. This led to a belief in the anthropic principle.

The Anthropic Principle

The anthropic principle assumes that a superhuman intelligence was involved in the creation of the universe. This principle is further divided into a weak anthropic principle and a strong anthropic principle, depending on the degree of involvement of that superhuman intelligence. The weak anthropic principle acknowledges that a superhuman intelligence was involved in determining the age of the universe and the position of the solar system but no more than that. By figuring out the structure of the universe, we can try to clarify why this involvement was essential.

The strong anthropic principle goes even further and posits that the physical principles and laws that govern the state of the universe were determined according to what is expedient for humans. If humans had never looked up at the sky, we may not have known whether the universe exists. Well might we ask the question, "Does the moon exist when no one is looking at it?"

How would you answer this question?

Even if the moon does not appear to exist when you are not looking at it, whether it actually exists is another matter. In fact, this question is the chief preoccupation of Mahayana Buddhism philosophy. According to this philosophy, the universe and everything in it belong to an empty void, and what we see are the products of different levels in our mind. Because there is only the void, human beings believe that they can change the world using the mind. This idea of the void or emptiness is fundamental to Buddhist beliefs.

The theory of the multiverse, on the other hand, as I mentioned earlier, claims that there is not only one universe; multiple universes exist. However, because the conditions and laws that govern those universes are so different from those in our universe, we are unable to access them.

The multiverse theory cannot be proved through experimentation, but we can use particle physics and mathematics to prove the potential for multiple universes to exist. Leading cosmologists are seriously pursuing this theory now. The multidimensional universe and superstring theories are examples of this.

Our Human Ancestry

As I mentioned, life appeared on Earth 3.8 billion years ago. However, our human ancestors evolved from animals no more than about seven million years ago. Life appeared first as fine prokaryotic (unicellular) cells, such as bacteria. These organisms then evolved into eukaryotic cells (more complex cells with nuclei), which merged and eventually became marine organisms. These, in turn, evolved into amphibians, then reptiles, which transformed into dinosaurs and birds and, eventually, mammals. From the subhuman primate, a new species branched out, becoming apes and finally evolving into Homo sapiens.

In humans, it takes about nine months for the fetus to grow inside the mother's body. Interestingly, in the first stage of this growth, the fetus resembles a fish. This is followed by a stage when it has the characteristics of an amphibian; then the characteristics of a reptile; then those of a mammal, until finally it takes on a human shape. This theory of comparative embryology was expressed by the *recapitulation theory*, which posits that the development of advanced species passes through stages represented by adult organisms of more primitive species.

A genetic comparison between chimpanzees and modern humans shows a 98 percent match. Early monkeys would have lived in trees in the same way as modern monkeys do. Somewhere along the line, a small genetic alteration in the monkey genes prompted a dramatic transformation. Our ancestors achieved this new evolution through the extraordinary development of our mental functions. As a result, these primates descended from the trees, started to walk on two legs, and began their evolution into our human ancestors. They used fire fearlessly and fashioned objects that would be useful in their everyday lives, such as earthenware and clothing. The human mind then focused on acquiring knowledge of the things and conditions of this world so that humans could make their lives easier and more convenient. Life appeared on Earth because of the miraculous conditions that existed, but life on Earth was far from easy.

Living organisms were born under the heavy restriction that they could not live long in the world. In order to survive, they needed to ingest nutrition from the outside environment in the form of food so that they could continually rebuild cells and tissue in their bodies. Therefore, eating and looking for food became the priority for living things. Indeed, moles, for example, will die in a single day if they do not find something to eat.

It takes energy to search for food and then digest it in order to rebuild the body. As a result, rest and sleep also became essential. The staple food of koalas in Australia is eucalyptus leaves, and digestion requires a large amount of energy, which tires them out. That is why they sleep for twenty-two hours a day. Humans had to make similar efforts to survive.

It is also important to note that the earth's environment was, and is, constantly changing; for example, during the ice age glaciers covered the surface of the earth, which melted during the warmer periods. This ice age lasted about one hundred thousand years, while the warmer period lasted for about ten thousand years. When the Holocene Ice Age ended, we entered the interglacial period. However, this interglacial period has lasted for more than ten thousand years, so it would not be surprising if the next ice age were to begin. Recently, however, the impact of global warming has become more pronounced, which makes it more difficult to predict the future.

During the ice age and the interglacial period, the temperature rose from five to ten degrees, and the sea level also changed, with the maximum disparity known to be over one hundred meters. During these changes, landmasses sink beneath the ocean, or are covered in deep glaciers, or join each other to form bigger landmasses, or new mountain ranges are formed. These transformations in the earth's environment continue to occur. For example, around ten thousand years ago, Asia and North America formed a single landmass, and humans were able to migrate between Asia and the Americas on foot.

Our ancestors had to cope with and adapt to these upheavals in the environment in order to survive. In fact, this world was never an ideal environment for human beings—to an almost absurd extent. Natural disasters such as earthquakes, tsunamis, typhoons, floods, and lightning cruelly and indiscriminately injure or kill people, including innocent children. While we need to eat to survive, food such as nuts, fish, and forest animals were not always readily available. We needed a way to survive in this kind of world.

The strategy adopted by the new species that became our human ancestors was to develop the brain and mind; they learned to concentrate their mental faculties to become knowledgeable about the things of the world and how they work, so that they could avert disasters or mitigate the damage they caused. This strategy was successful, and humans started to make clothing to cope with cold and heat, learned how to vary foodstuff by cooking in earthenware pots, and steadily improved their lives by building houses instead of sleeping in caves. The biggest change to their lives was wrought by the introduction of agriculture.

Agricultural production made it possible to produce more grain and food than necessary for daily life. That paved the way for us to live in groups, and society was born. This surplus of food gave birth to the notion of ownership, requiring power and organization to determine who owned the food and who decided how to use it. The fire of human desires was lit.

This fire of human desire grew and spread in all directions. The objects of our desire were not only wealth and property or precious stones; we began to also desire intangible things until a great gap opened between the rich and poor, creating discrimination. This brought with it the desire to be superior to others, to stand above and rule over them.

When desires collide, conflicts arise. A clash in the desire stakes between countries results in war. We try to find a compromise to avoid this, but more often, negotiations are carried out against a background of force, and desires such as patriotism, pride, and religious beliefs interfere. People often try to change their situation by trumpeting their ideals. The banner of the French Revolution was freedom, equality, and fraternity, but the victorious revolutionaries carried out a bloody purge by ruthlessly killing their enemies and suppressing them with force. The freedom, equality, and fraternity they lauded applied only to themselves.

Communism also drew on the ideals of the French Revolution and the notion of equality. However, in the Soviet Union and China, Stalin and Mao Zedong mercilessly repressed the opposition and behaved as dictators. The European Union (EU) also inherited some of these ideals, but they too are seriously undermined by the threatened departure of the UK from the union. To understand why these events occurred, we need to know more about the nature of humans and the workings of the mind.

The Food Chain and Its Mysteries

The existence of the food chain helps us to understand life in this world. All living things must eat to survive, but in the main, this food is obtained by killing and eating other creatures. Organisms on earth are chained to one another through the act of eating something smaller than themselves or being eaten by something bigger than themselves, until we reach human beings, who are at the top of this food chain. Human beings are physically small and weak, but we have become the strongest and most invincible power on earth, using the weapons and technologies created with our minds— like a God ruling over all.

Killing and eating other creatures to survive may appear as an act of cruelty. Many people see our world as a place where only the fittest survive and live their lives accordingly. On the other hand, some people avoid the cruelty of killing animals by becoming vegetarians and strongly believe that animals such as dolphins and whales, with higher intelligence, should be protected. However, there is no escaping the fact that nature is based on the food chain.

Animals often lay more eggs than necessary, and plants will spread an overabundance of seeds and fruits that can be eaten by other living things. In this way, the food chain keeps the ecosystem of the entire planet in balance. Moreover, animals do not kill more than is necessary. Once the animal's appetite has been satiated by eating another animal, it will not go on to attack new prey until it is hungry again. Only human beings are completely ruthless toward other creatures. In exchange for developing the mind, human beings have sacrificed that animal instinct of when to stop, and as a result, humans are capable of infinite cruelty. Our food is now mass produced in the form of food factories such as large-scale poultry and pig farms. These farming methods are often cruel to the animals, as large groups of them are confined in small spaces so that they can be fattened with the least amount of effort and expense.

The food chain principle is applicable even with the evolution of the two types of biological cells I mentioned earlier, the eukaryotic and prokaryotic cells. Prokaryotic cells are unicellular, while eukaryotic cells are multiple prokaryotic cells combined. The transformation of prokaryotic organisms into eukaryote organisms was the first step in evolution. However, why prokaryotic cells evolved into eukaryotic cells is still a major mystery in biology. The prevailing theory is that larger prokaryotic cells capture and eat small prokaryotic bacteria, which for some reason, instead of dying, continue to live after being ingested, thereby forming a symbiotic relationship from which eukaryotic cells were born.

The act of eating involves ingesting another organism in order to rebuild and strengthen from the inside. On the other hand, to be ingested is to give up existence and become a part of the other so that the other can grow. While this can explain the metabolic function of living things, the more interesting notion to explore is that when these small cells are ingested, they do not die but rather form this symbiotic relationship with the consumer. Something similar happens when humans eat meat, vegetables, or fish, for example. These enter the body, but rather than "dying," they too form a symbiotic relationship with us.

This food we eat contains within it a range of energies— or life forces—that are undamaged by the preparation and cooking process. Instead, they continue to live on inside of us—in symbiosis with us, so to speak. They promote within us an energy and a range of actions that are indispensable to human life in this world. The workings of these life forces will be explained in more detail in a later chapter.

The belief that spirits exist in everything that inhabits the world is called animism, and many civilizations have supported and continue to support this idea. Despite this fact, animism is dismissed outright when the theory of evolution is taught as a major part of school curricula. Animism is treated as a primitive religion or a set of superstitions that belonged to an era when human intelligence was underdeveloped. According to this theory of evolution, religion began with animism, evolved into polytheism, and eventually transformed into monotheistic beliefs such as Judaism, Christianity, and Islam. Is this really the case?

Take, for example, the customs of the Ainu, Japan's indigenous people, which embody animism and incorporate the idea of the food chain. The Ainu hunt and eat bears, but they also worship them as the incarnation of a god. The Ainu belief is that the god becomes flesh so that it can be eaten by humans and sustain life. The Ainu give thanks to this god through ritual bear festivals. The killing of the bear is not considered an act of cruelty. To eat the flesh of the bear is to absorb the life of the bear inside oneself, thereby continuing one's own life in an act of gratitude to the god for his self-sacrifice. Nothing separates man from bear, and this belief gives new meaning to the idea of the food chain. When the bear is killed and eaten, the Ainu recognize that it does not lose its life but rather lives on and coexists inside the body of the person who eats it. Many similar animistic beliefs exist within more hierarchical forms of religion practiced today.

The Unknown Being of Man

While there is no doubt that science has given us enormous benefits, it is not without drawbacks. Our lives have become more convenient and easier, with vast new possibilities open to us. However, we cannot deny that there are limitations to these scientific methodologies and the observations based on them.

Eighty years ago, Alexis Carrel, a French physician and medical scientist, won the Nobel Prize in Physiology or Medicine and wrote a book that became a worldwide bestseller. The title of the book is *Man, the Unknown* (*L'Homme, cet Inconnu*), and in it, Carrel criticized modern civilization and the scientific worldview and pointed out that we still know nothing about humans.

The book was translated into eighteen languages, and a total of ten million copies were sold around the world. However, Carrel was heavily criticized after his death for supporting eugenics—the desire to create superior humans through heredity—and cooperating with the Nazis. His name became taboo, and his influence waned.

I remember reading Carrel's book when I was a young man. Some of the ideas he expressed made a big impression on me, and

I mention them here not with the intention of recommending the book. In the eighty years since its publication, science has made huge advancements and transformed our lives. However, to me, the title of this book, suggesting there is so much about humans that we do not know, is a fitting thought for our times.

As a young man, Carrel taught at Lyon University, and one day he decided to visit the Fountain of Lourdes, famous for the miraculous healing of diseases by the Virgin Mary. As Carrel was a surgeon, he had intended to scientifically analyze how the waters of the fountain could miraculously cure disease. Instead, he witnessed the miraculous healing of a female patient who had travelled to Lourdes with him and to whom he had given the prognosis that she would die within days. By that stage, her stomach was swollen with end-stage tuberculosis peritonitis. Within minutes of her arrival at the fountain, however, all her symptoms disappeared, and, astonishingly, her body was returned to health.

Carrel was shaken and confused by the conflict he then experienced between his faith and the common sense of a scientist. After much anguish, he chose faith and a dormant sense of hope over a conclusion based on science and reason. He wrote about the realities he had witnessed and his resulting mental conflict in a memoir that he was too hesitant to publish. In the end, it was published by his wife after his death.

Science has given us a vast amount of knowledge, but this knowledge has become more and more fragmented, increasingly specialized and harder to understand. The outcome is an increasingly grimmer outlook. Science deals with the explanation of phenomena, but every time something is explained, a new mystery is born from a part of that explanation. That part is further broken down into smaller units in order to explain the new mystery, but that in turn gives birth to another mystery, and this process is infinitely repeated. While it is important to solve all the smaller mysteries that arise, we need a grand design or a blueprint to see the whole picture. Without it, we will easily lose our way, like a traveler who is lost in a deep forest or a sailor who rows out into the ocean but loses all sense of direction, despite the fact that the nearby waves, rocks, and islands are visible. The following section discusses some of the failings of scientific discoveries in the past.

Examples of Scientific Beliefs Upended

Recently, scientific studies have overturned many long-held beliefs that were socially accepted as scientific creed. The most shocking of these discoveries was the emergence of quantum theory (also known as particle physics or quantum mechanics).

The theories of Newton, famous for his discovery of gravity, dominated physics for the second half of the seventeenth century. For more than two hundred years, scientists claimed that the smallest unit of matter was the atom; science was convinced this was the case, and therefore people believed it. However, toward the end of the nineteenth century and early twentieth century, the discovery of elementary particles called electrons revealed that this was not the truth. Atoms are made up of a nucleus in the center and electrons that fly around the nucleus. Scientists discovered that an electron is a type of elementary particle, and an atomic nucleus is a collection of elementary particles. Instead of atoms being the smallest units of matter, it was discovered that elementary particles were even smaller than atoms. This discovery gave birth to quantum theory, or particle physics, which attempts to understand these properties. This heralded the study of elementary particles that turned out to be a strange new world we could never have imagined—a world where elementary particles can be both particles and waves at the same time.

When the nature of electrons was examined, it was discovered that rather than being passively attracted to the nucleus and orbiting it as dead particles, electrons can freely exit the orbit to fly around. These were called free electrons. Interestingly, when Bapak, the founder of Subud, heard about this discovery, he realized it supported his own observations that matter is alive and constantly changing, and while it is subject to many restrictions, it can also influence the objects around it—but more of that later.

Science defines matter as a collection of solid particles. These solid particles have *locality* in that they occupy a specific place in space at a specific time. If something else attempts to enter that place, it will be blocked by the existing occupant. This property of matter is somewhat similar to how humans build fences and walls and lock doors to keep robbers out.

Waves, on the other hand, have no locality. The waves that we actually see and hear, such as the ripples of water, the waves of the sea, or sounds heard in our ears, are not actually waves themselves but vibrations of water and air, which are media that transmit waves in the physical world. It takes time for vibrations to be transmitted a long way because these media have resistance, and so over time and space, the vibrations gradually lose strength and eventually disappear.

Elementary particles do not use matter for wave transmission because they themselves have the nature of waves. These waves are not visible to us because the human eye cannot see anything that is not matter. These waves are thought to spread out infinitely and invisibly in a vacuum. While it has not been possible to confirm the truth of this, an electron gun experiment—called the double-slit experiment—has shown how these elementary particles also share the nature of waves.

In this experiment, an electron gun is used to produce and fire individual electrons at a screen placed in front of a wall. The screen has two parallel slits, and if the electrons fired at the screen are solid particles, they should pass through one of the slits and hit the wall on the other side, leaving traces on the wall. However, what happens instead is that the fired electrons pass through both slits and hit the wall in a striped pattern that is characteristic of wave-specific resonance. Originally, it was not thought possible that these individual electrons could collide and interfere with themselves to produce wavelike resonance. In this case, however, the impossible appears to have become possible. The human mind is not capable of understanding how matter can simultaneously possess the two incompatible properties of solid particles that have locality and waves that do not. It gets even stranger, however, when you look at the behavior of elementary particles. These particles act like waves when they are not being observed, but as soon as an attempt is made to detect them, they no longer appear to be waves but exhibit the properties of particles. Once they become particles, it is possible to grasp their locality and their movements.

A further astonishing discovery was *quantum entanglement*, whereby a pair of elementary particles become linked so that no matter how far away they are from each other, their spin (the direction of their angle of rotation) is instantly communicated to each other. If one particle changes their spin direction, the other particle changes their spin direction relative to this at the same moment. These particles could exist at either end of the universe and yet still communicate instantly—even faster than the speed of light.

The world of elementary particles concerns sizes that are less than one thousandth of a centimeter. If elementary particles were as big as human beings, our bodies would be as large as the entire universe. The events in this micro world, therefore, do not directly appear to affect our lives in the macro world, but they do have relevance. All matter in this world consists of conglomerations of elementary particles. Indeed, matter that is larger than elementary particles but shows the same properties as elementary particles has been discovered.

The more we discover about the world of elementary particles, the closer we get to a paradigm shift. Quantum physics is already a typical example of how existing scientific theories were comprehensively overturned by the same science that produced them. Indeed, quantum theory has become the new classical physics.

The next example of a similar overthrow of scientific theory occurred in 2012 with the astronomical discovery of dark matter and dark energy in the universe. Scientists have consistently claimed that everything that exists in the universe is matter. They analyzed matter and measured the energy of its constituent elements. There are forces that attract, such as gravity, and forces that repel. If all the forces of energy that exist in the universe are added together, the result produces the total amount of energy. Scientists calculated this; however, the question remained: if nothing exists in the universe except matter, why does the universe continue to expand as it is doing? Further research was needed, and this led to the discovery of something that science cannot fully explain—namely, the existence of dark matter. Dark matter forces the universe of mass and gravity to contract, but it exists alongside another unknown force, that of dark energy, which acts to expand the universe.

NASA released the figures below that show the proportions of matter, dark matter, and dark energy in the universe.

- The ratio of matter to the entire universe is 5 percent.

- The ratio of dark matter to the entire universe is 27 percent.

- The ratio of dark energy to the entire universe is 68 percent.

In other words, the proportion of matter is less than 10 percent of the universe, and the remainder is an unknown energy that is not identifiable by today's science. NASA's announcement was as much a surprise to scientists as it was to the general public.

The ultimate example of a scientific belief being turned on its head was revealed in a program produced by NHK, Japan's public broadcaster. For several years, NHK has been dispatching research teams to various countries for its special series, *The Body*. This series reports on the latest advancements in medicine around the world. Between the fall of 2017 and the spring of 2018, NHK aired a special edition of the series in seven episodes, *The Body: Our Remarkable Inner Network*. Professor Shinya Yamanaka of Kyoto University, a world-renowned scientist who won the Nobel Prize in Physiology or Medicine in 2012, also participated in the broadcast as a commentator.

The program set out to fundamentally reverse a theory that had been unquestioned until then. Previously, science had taught that the human brain acts like the body's command tower, issuing instructions to all the organs in the body. This puts the brain at the center of everything. All parts of the body and our organs are connected to the brain through a neural network and work according to directives from the brain.

Besides the brain, it has been known for many years that hormones have an effect on the functioning of the organs. Hormones are produced by specific organs and delivered into the bloodstream, where they affect the entire body. Prominent among these are the sex hormones produced in the genitals, the corticosteroids produced by the kidneys, and the thyroid hormones produced by the thyroid gland. The brain also regulates the production of hormones by signaling to the organs the quantities to produce, and in this respect, it retains control. What was newly discovered was the fact that each organ produces hormonelike substances independently of the brain and passes these into the blood. Other organs receive information from these substances, and this determines their subsequent action. They send this new information back into the blood. Since these hormonelike substances did not have a formal name, NHK named them "message substances." The organs in the body interact with one another by exchanging these message substances. Research over the past few decades has revealed the existence of several thousands of these message substances.

This discovery means that the organs create and use a vast network of information independently of the brain. What is even more surprising is that this information network also exists within a single cell, like a blueprint at a molecular level. This surprising theory has not been proposed by just one or two scientists but is the result of advanced medical research from a great many laboratories that continue to report on this. The information was first broadcast in Japan, and a Japanese medical scientist was instrumental in its discovery after he found that the heart produces a substance similar to a hormone. There is a growing expectation that we will begin to discover more and more similar facts about the body in the near future.

In this section, we started with the world of very fine elementary particles, then moved to the opposite extreme of the cosmic universe, finishing up with the human body. In each of these cases, we saw how scientific convictions were turned on their head by the same science that discovered them. In a recent television interview, Dr. Akira Yoshino, a professional scientist who won the Nobel Prize in Chemistry in 2019, mentioned that while young students think science has already explained everything there is to know, in fact, scientists know less than 1 or 2 percent of everything there is to know!

Dr. Yoshino may have said this to encourage young people to take up the challenge of science, but at the same time, he was expressing his opinion that since we only understand between 1 and 2 percent of the entire mystery of the universe, any scientific belief can be overturned at any time.

CHAPTER 2

MUHAMMAD SUBUH'S NEW INSIGHT

The Function of the Mind and the Latihan

Muhammad Subuh, usually known as Bapak, is the founder of the Subud movement. Although Bapak is no longer alive, Subud has spread around the world and is now present in more than eighty countries. At the heart of Subud is the Latihan, which is an unprecedented and deeply mysterious form of spiritual training. This training of the Latihan was created by Bapak and did not exist before then.

Bapak was a young Indonesian man, only twenty-four years old, when he first experienced this training of the Latihan in 1925. It came to him as a sphere of brilliant light that entered his head from above and caused his body to vibrate intensely. His body was filled with a strange power as though it had become transparent and was brightly illuminated from within. Parts of his body began to move without being willed. Over the following one thousand nights, he had similarly intense experiences that revealed to him the vast breadth and depth of this practice. This was the start of Latihan in the world.

Strangely enough, although these experiences kept him up all night, he was able to rise in the morning and go to his work as usual. There was no one who could explain to him what all of this meant, but gradually he came to understand the significance and purpose of the movements of his body in Latihan. The involuntary movements he found himself making were a physical manifestation of the contact between his human soul and the Great Life Force of the creative power of God. Through the contact of the Latihan, the power of God flows into the soul, initiating a purification of the mind and body. The act of accepting the promptings of this unknown force in the body and obeying it unconditionally represents an act of worship of God by the human soul.

To explain further, the process of purification starts in the parts of the body and the senses. Then it moves inside so that the emotional functions, then the thought functions, and eventually the consciousness itself are all gradually purified. As a result, the physical and mental impurities that attach to our bodies and minds are wiped away, and we are able to return to our state of original purity and live in a way that is appropriate to a true human being. For this reason, the process takes time.[1]

With this new spiritual training of the Latihan, Bapak

---

[1] For a more in-depth description of the Latihan state, its purpose and significance, and the different phases of purification, see my previous book, *Latihan: A Path to Great Life and a New Way to Purify the Soul.*

brought us fresh insight into the human condition. He particularly stressed the special nature of the human mind. The chief function of the mind is to think, and Bapak pointed out that human thought has an affinity with matter. We can use our thoughts to control material objects and freely create tools and devices that make our lives easier. We use language to communicate our thoughts. Over many decades, people in the West regarded emotions as inferior to thought. They viewed intelligence and reason as pure and objective—free from the influence of emotion and fantasy—and therefore the optimal way to connect to the wisdom of God. This is perhaps one explanation for the status of men and women in Western culture, where men were identified with reason and women with emotion. It has only been in recent years that this prejudice has been addressed.

This emphasis on reasoning and its integral relationship with language was expressed in the Bible. In the first chapter of his Gospel, John writes: "In the beginning was the Word, and the Word was with God, and the Word was God. Through him all things were made; without him nothing was made that has been made. In him was life, and that life was the light of all mankind."[1]

Bapak suggested that the "all things" mentioned here are limited to things of this world and our perception of them and that human thought is of no use as a means to understand spiritual truth. He added that it is our minds that prevent us from perceiving or sensing the existence of God and His power. The mind is a function of the brain and, as such, is an integral part of the body. We can only perceive things through our minds, and yet this sets up an extra filter that obscures our vision of spiritual realities.

Said to be the founder of early modern philosophy, the seventeenth-century French philosopher René Descartes said, "I think, therefore I am," and this idea is still firmly believed to be what defines being human. One of his contemporaries, Blaise Pascal, a great scientist, mathematician, and philosopher and well known for his Pascal's theorem and Pascal's principle, also said, "Thought constitutes the greatness of man." This idea that what defines a human is their ability to think is still a commonly held belief. Bapak's definition of the mind is somewhat contrary to this belief but cannot be fully understood without relating it to the Latihan in Subud. We can reach a clearer understanding of this idea if we look at the history of how our minds developed historically as well as through the process of birth and growth.

The Evolution of the Mind

To better adapt to the world's environment, living organisms had to evolve slowly over centuries. Our human ancestors attempted to shorten this time by developing their minds, using materials to make tools, and expanding and strengthening their innate abilities. This is something humans continue to do; we created objects such as microscopes to make microscopic organisms visible, telescopes to view distant space, and prosthetic limbs to enable movement for people who had lost their own. Inventions such as these require an accurate knowledge of materials in the world. Our ancestors sharpened the functions of their minds and sensory organs to gain knowledge of the material world. Our sensory organs—the eyes, the ears, the nose, the mouth, and skin—connect us to the external world. However, in the process of training our minds to better understand the world, we learned to ignore and negate anything that was not visible to us. Bapak suggested that the mind cannot know spiritual truth; we cannot experience God or the spiritual universe through our minds. He saw that the Latihan was given to humankind as a special grace from God, to rescue us from this state of unknowing.

Humans are not good at controlling our own minds. We do, however, possess an inner sense that can bypass the five senses to receive information directly from the soul. While this inner sense was once able to exert some control over our minds, this ability has declined over time, and its function was compromised. In the process of evolution, we developed the organs and functions of the body that proved most useful in improving life in this world. Those that proved less useful eventually weakened and disappeared. In this way, this inner sense ceased to have importance and gradually declined.

Historically, many truth seekers were aware that thought hinders our knowledge of spiritual truths. They attempted to minimize the involvement of their thoughts through meditation. Specifically, this was done in ways such as focusing the mind on a single image, such as the Buddha's likeness or a mandala, or chanting mantras in order to drive out all thought. However, this is not a fully satisfactory solution. Thoughts may be suppressed through willpower, but this willpower itself is a kind of thought. We have no other means of achieving these aims except through thought. To understand Bapak's point about the inability of the mind to experience spiritual truth, we need to take a closer look at the nature of the human mind.

The Nature of the Mind

The chief functions of the mind are thought and emotion; these are also supported by a range of affiliated functions. Significant among these are the faculty of memory and the ability to use language to express our state of mind. These faculties have allowed human beings to live together in societies, thereby bringing about culture and civilization. Our desires and our will set the direction we need to move in, while our thoughts and emotions provide us with the energy we need to move in that direction. In addition, our five sensory organs, though they do not belong to the mind, act like relatives who cooperate with the actions of the mind.

It takes nine months for a baby to grow inside the mother's body. When the baby is born, it is furnished with all the functions of the mind, but it does not understand their content yet. The newborn can hold things and suckle at its mother's breast; it has the faculty of memory yet remembers nothing; the ability to speak, yet it has no words. It has eyes and ears but cannot see or hear much for a few days after its birth. However, as soon as the newborn's five senses start to work, they begin to collect content for the mind. Babies begin to look at their hands and their feet and move them about. This gives them awareness of their own body. They start to lick things to see if they taste good or bad, and they start to express their emotions through crying, movements, and facial expressions.

The knowledge that babies acquire and remember is all limited to things of this world. When they come across anything new, they make a judgment about it by innately comparing it with content that has already been collected by their mind. In fact, this approach stays with us throughout our lives. In the last thirty years or so, research into the behavior of babies has uncovered extraordinary abilities in the newborn infant, such as their ability to mimic the movements of the parents' mouth and hands. Just one hour after birth, newborns, who were thought to be mostly blind, were shown to be already capable of mimicking facial movements. This type of mimicking is a complex act; the baby must observe the expression of its parent and then move the muscles of its face in the same way. We now know that newborns can distinguish the voice of their mother from that of other women, as the fetus listens to sounds and voices from the external world while in the womb. Some infants even remember these sounds up until the age of three or four.

Initially, scientists dismissed these observed phenomena

as imagination. To Bapak, however, these were true memories because while the baby is a fetus or newly born, it is still in touch with the spiritual world through its own soul, from which it receives information. The newborn is unable to see or hear well, yet it occasionally smiles or wears a sad expression as though reacting to information from its soul.

As we grow older, we lose contact with our souls. Children who had mysterious abilities as infants forget about them once they turn three or four years old. All of us forget our babyhood. In general, people determine whether things are true or false by comparing them with the existing content of their minds. If the mind finds nothing against which to measure that object, it will ignore it. This is also true of the spiritual experience of babies. As babies start to become aware of the things of this world and absorb this knowledge, their minds are filled with content that comes only from the world, and they start to forget their spiritual experience.

The spiritual universe created by God is governed directly by God and the power of God. However, we are incapable of perceiving that reality. We do not have the ability to recognize a world that is infinitely more delicate and sophisticated than the material world. We can only develop a keener awareness of this after our understanding has been cleansed. The mind perceives only the things of this world—just as in quantum theory, where elementary particles transform into waves and become invisible as soon as we try to observe them.

The Engine of Desire That Drives Thought

Historically, intelligence and reason have been considered to be superior faculties—objective forms of thought unaffected by emotions or imagination. However, as forms of thought, can we truly say they are independent and objective? No one can definitively answer in the positive. People will often change their minds in response to changing circumstances. This offers flexibility, but it is also unreliable, as we saw in the previous chapter with the examples of deeply held scientific beliefs being completely overturned. The Book of Changes, from ancient China, offers the phrase, *A wise man changes his mind*. Despite this ability to adapt, many people will also stick stubbornly to their own ideas, even if circumstances around them change, because of the fixedness of their desires and their will.

Our desires and our will give energy to our thoughts. Underlying this is the intense desire to stay alive. We do not want to die because we do not know what death is. We think that death means to lose the human body and the existence of the self. Our desire for life is as deep and wide as the roots of giant trees. From this strong desire spring myriads of other desires, which become intertwined like the branches. When these desires surface, they take the form of impulses that dominate all other thoughts or concerns. Humans cannot escape this reality. These desires are the testament of the instinct to survive embedded in humans since they were created as living beings in this world. The object of these desires is the wish to live comfortably in this world, more specifically, in line with the premise of wealth and good health. Accordingly, people are impatient to acquire these. Thinking is not the master of desire but becomes its servant; the inevitable result is that desire and the force of our will direct the activities of the mind.

It follows that we cannot control our minds by ourselves, and since the driving force of the mind is our desires, this also means that we cannot control our desires. It might look like the will controls desire, but it only manages to control part of our desires—not all of them. People think they can control their minds through willpower, but the will also belongs to the mind. This control may strengthen some part of the mind, but this serves to weaken another part of the mind. In the end, it is still controlled by the mind. We are fully released from the activities of the mind only when the brain, the parent of the mind, ceases to function, or the body dies. However, even when the body dies, the mind of the person is carried over to the world after death and continues to exist. The will, thoughts, and emotions that are the content of the mind are not objects but more like information in the form of spiritual waves.

Of course, there is a big difference in the state of mind before and after death. The body, which was the source of energy for the mind's activity, ceases to exist after death, and when the mind is transported to the afterworld, it is therefore fixed in the state it was in at death. Bapak also said that the mind remains locked after death, and its content cannot be revoked, altered, or added to. This means that when asked after you die what you did in this life, you cannot bend the facts, lie, or make excuses. There is no hiding in the spiritual world ruled by God and his power.

Humans and Angels

In the physical world, human beings can lie, deceive, cheat, and go back on their word. The physical and chemical laws that govern the universe represent the indirect rule of God, whereas the spiritual world is ruled directly by God. In the material world, only the physical body and its actions are recognized as real. Since the mind that is behind these actions is not seen as a material reality, we can think however we like, lie however we like, and this alone does not constitute a crime. Humans are given godlike freedom along with free will; we are permitted to do anything so long as it does not violate these laws. This is a freedom that even the angels would envy. So much so that we can act out of a love that is beyond the angels, or we can act without mercy in ways that even the devil would hesitate to.

The reason why humans were given such great freedom, Bapak suggests, is as a result of God's fairness. Angels and human beings are both God's creatures, but because angels are made of light, they do not fall ill, grow old, or die. The human body is made of matter; it is exposed to cold and heat, easily sickens, and grows old and dies. This seems less fair, and so to strike a balance, humans were given greater freedom. This means we can exercise our free will, use our thinking minds to judge right from wrong, and attempt anything we wish. However, this ability to think is limited to the pursuit of things of this world and becomes a useless tool for understanding spiritual truths.

Bapak's View of Our Place in the Spiritual Universe

In Bapak's view, the spiritual universe is composed of seven different levels of life forces, and each possesses a different nature and has within it the desire to remain alive. Together, these seven levels, or worlds, make up the greater cosmos, which continues to evolve as a single life force.

The layers of this cosmic universe consist of three lower-order worlds, which are the animal world, the vegetable world, and the material world; the human world in the center; and three higher-order worlds above the human world, as listed below.

1. The material life force
2. The vegetable life force
3. The animal life force
4. The ordinary human life force
5. The Roh Rohani life force of the complete human being
6. The Roh Rachmani higher life force that represents compassion
7. The Roh Rabanni life force that represents creativity

Surrounding this universe and penetrating through these

layers are the two forces that come directly from the power of God. These two forces are known as the Roh Ilofi and the Roh Kudus. The Roh Ilofi, or Great Life Force, is the creative power of God, and it penetrates all of existence in the universe and allows passage between the levels that would otherwise be inaccessible. The second force is the Roh Kudus, which is the power of the angels. Angels, who are God's servants, are composed of light from God, and this power envelops the universe from outside it. These latter two forces are made up of elements of light.

The Subud symbol represents this spiritual universe as seven concentric circles, which Bapak suggested was easier to understand if we imagine it in a three-dimensional view. This seven-layered universe is presented as a series of concentric circles whereby each higher-order level envelops the one beneath it, and these circles are all divided by seven radial spokes that represent the Great Life Force.

The human world is located at the center of this hierarchy, three levels from the bottom and three from the top. This position means we can be pulled in either direction—down toward the three lower-order worlds or up toward the three higher-order worlds. These seven life forces are like waveforms that are finer or coarser, depending on whether they are higher or lower, and they operate in accordance with the desires of that level, and these desires that we experience are evidence that they exist.

These various forces differ in nature depending on their

wavelengths, just as sunlight is reflected in different colors depending on the wavelength of the light. It is therefore impossible to enter or interact with these forces unless you are of the same wavelength. Since the human body is formed by the three lower-order forces, we are continually exposed to the waveforms of desire of those forces. When these forces influence the mind, our thoughts and actions manifest the characteristics of those desires.

The Soul and the Life Forces

The cause of this unique situation is that when God created us, He determined that the soul should be what commands us. The content of our souls should be that of the Roh Rohani life force, which is a level higher than the human level and represents the complete human being. At the same time, our bodies were formed from the material of this world. The Bible states that God created humans from dust and breathed life into us. This means that the origin and true home of the human soul is not earth but the world of Roh Rohani. After death, when the material body is lost, the Roh Rohani becomes the soul's goal and destination. However, as long as the body exists as matter, it contains within it the life forces of the human level and the three below. These forces are spiritual life forms, and they continue to live with us and serve us by producing the various energies needed to live in this world.

The human ability to think is not independent; the life

forces that exist within the mind make use of this faculty to fulfill their own desires. Since these life forces are below the level of humans, the objects of their desires are limited to the profits of this material world, and they have no relationship with the spiritual world beyond the human. However, because human beings have within their souls the content of a higher life force, we can also experience a higher order of thought. Bapak described the relationship between the life forces and our thoughts as that of oil to a lamp's flame. The oil of a lamp is like the energy of the life forces—their desire for life. The flame is like the thought created by the energy of the oil. If the quality of the oil is good, the flame will shine brightly. If the quality is poor, the flame will be dark and clouded.

The quality of the "oil" depends on the life forces within a person's soul and what stage they have reached. If the inner content of the soul is of a higher life force, as originally intended by God, that person's thoughts, like a bright flame, will light up not only their way but many people around them also. However, if the content of the soul is filled with the material life force, that person's thoughts will become like a dark and clouded flame, and their behavior will also take on an inhuman nature.

Bapak indicated that the spiritual quality of children is not necessarily homogeneous with that of their parents, as this also depends on the passions, thoughts, and feelings of their parents when they came together to create that child. The soul acts as a command center and is also itself a vessel.

The spiritual life forces enter the soul, which comes to life and takes up its role as a command center. The life force that will enter the child's soul is not predetermined but depends on the state of the mind of the man and woman at the time of their union and their attitudes in daily life. If the inner state of the parent is completely material, a soul imbued with the material life force that is waiting for rebirth will be called from the afterworld to become that child. That is why, Bapak explained, sometimes parents of noble character and discernment have unhappy children who do not resemble them. This explanation by Bapak is unusual and may be difficult for people to accept right away.

The Desires of the Life Forces and How They Are Manifest

Among the seven life forces, the material, vegetable, and animal life forces are of special importance to us. These life forces enter us as food and survive regardless of how we cook or prepare them, because they are spiritual entities that coexist with us, supporting and helping our lives. Most of our bodies are the product of the vegetable life force, while the material and other life forces give us the motivation and the energy we need to live our lives. The chief function of the mind—the ability to think—has an affinity with the material life force, and for that reason, human beings can freely exploit material objects and the scientific laws that govern them. This allows us to make objects useful for our lives, such as clothing, furniture, and houses, or to construct buildings, nuclear power plants, and spaceships.

Bapak spoke of our indebtedness to these lower forces for helping us to live in this world, and the need to repay this debt by helping them to return to their rightful homes when we return to our soul's home after death. I recall an occasion when Bapak described these lower forces to Subud members as follows. He said that the lower life forces act in accordance with the desires of that level, and each of them has their own color. The material life force desires are the color of the nature of matter, and the vegetable life force desires are the color of the nature of plants. If a person is too much under the influence of those desires, their way of thinking and feeling will reflect those colors accordingly. Eventually, they will experience negative and corrupt thoughts and feelings that they cannot control. This is where the thinking ability we are so proud of proves not to be so useful. Thought is not the master of desire but has become its servant.

Matter is cold, completely self-centered, and thoroughly indifferent to others. People influenced by this material force desire try to keep everything to themselves; they want to be richer, smarter, and better than anyone else. They are characterized by greed, which is never satisfied no matter how much it acquires, anger, and arrogance. This person becomes arrogant or irritable when a selfish and greedy desire is unfulfilled or somehow hindered. This ends in trouble and contention. An example is someone whose pride is hurt and who becomes angry when a coworker is always lucky or gets promoted sooner than they do. Such a person treats other human beings as things and has no compunctions about behaving cruelly and ruthlessly.

The desire of the vegetable life force is for growth and self-expansion, and it spares no effort to achieve this. Plants, unlike matter, can have interrelationship but cannot move like animals, so their sphere of action remains narrow; this is limited to the extent to which direct touching or feeling is possible. Plants put roots down into the soil and extend upward in search of sunlight. A person influenced by the vegetable life force is a hard worker who spares no effort. Hard work is a good thing and a desirable quality for humans. However, a person who is strongly under the influence of the desire of the vegetable force has a narrow field of vision and remains attached to the village and land where they were born and raised. Even if their lives are hard, they passively accept this as their fate and never think they can find new possibilities by venturing out to the world outside. If competitors appear who threatens that person's growth, they see that person as the enemy and will use any means to defeat them. Since this level is close to that of the material life force, the affected person shares similarities with that force and thus will attempt to drag their opponent down.

Animals can roam freely and have a much wider living area than plants. However, they need to forage for food, such as leaves and nuts, and chase and catch prey that do their best to escape them. For that reason, animals and birds are usually curious about new things and attempt to possess everything they see. They often build territories to protect their nests and habitats. Driven by strong lust, they chase after the opposite sex, and for that reason are endowed with an enthusiasm and unshakeable endurance. Some animals have mates and children and thus form families. Some of these animals show affection and loyalty to their family members, creating a kind of social culture. In this way, the animal life force gives us the sense of adventure and pursuit and the endurance we need. Without these, it would be hard for us to overcome life's tough challenges. On the other hand, people who are dominated by the desire of the animal life force do not hesitate to act brutally and ruthlessly to achieve their goals. They may not kill without purpose, but they will make enemies of those who threaten their territory and fight them to the death. Some people become vegetarians for health or religious reasons, because they believe it is cruel to kill animals. Bapak suggested that the atmosphere and the plants we eat are full of microscopic creatures, such as bacteria and viruses, and we are thus consuming animal life forces continually without being aware of this.

To stay alive, humans must constantly replenish their bodies by rebuilding the cells inside it. That is why we have appetite and we find food delicious. From a spiritual viewpoint, however, this is much more than simply a physical, metabolic action. We think that the state of hunger derives purely from metabolic and chemical effects, but Bapak explained that our desire to eat and our experience of food being delicious arise from the existence of the lower forces within us. In order to survive within the human body, these life forces constantly seek to encounter and unite with identical life forces, not dissimilar to the desire for love and marriage in human beings. When we eat meat, vegetables, and fish, these life forces are alive and enter us through this food, and if they find a worthy partner, they feel delight, and consequently the eater finds the food delicious. If they do not find the right partner, the food tastes bad. The human body is built to have these feelings, and Bapak remarked that while animals, plants, and matter are from different levels and subject to different conditions, their way of thinking and feeling mean their lives are almost identical to the lives of human beings. Most scientists have an extreme aversion to anthropomorphism and see it as delusional. However, Bapak's assertion is not speculation or fantasy but is a direct recognition of the way of life of spiritual life forces.

As the three lower life forces enter our bodies through our food, we become aware of their effects. The life force of the ordinary human being, however, softens the negative aspects of those three life forces and gives us a human morality. This life force yields when yielding is necessary, preferring peace and harmony through discussion rather than fighting. It wants to help others, recognizes the existence of God, and tries to worship God. Therefore, it is a beneficial life force that humans need. However, this life force too has its drawbacks. It cannot be separated from self-interest, and this results in a tendency to prioritize intelligence above God. Trust in God is lessened, and the motivation to worship God weakened. Moreover, if the person does something wrong, they involve others around them in the problem for their own benefit. Seeing this behavior as wrong may also be unfair since self-interest is a necessary part of living in this world and is indeed proof of life. A world without this force is no longer a human world but a higher-order spiritual world that transcends the human level.

These worlds are linked to one another, but they are autonomous and cannot exchange freely with one another. Anything that does not share the same nature as a particular world cannot live in that world or interact with the things that exist in that world. Forcing oneself into another world will result only in pain and the desire to escape it.

Each of these levels is further divided into seven more areas, and each level also reflects the nature of all the other levels that are projected onto it. In this way, both the nature of the higher-order world superior to humans and the nature of the lower world below humans are projected onto our world. The degree of progression toward a higher force in each of those seven areas depends on which world it is reflecting. So, for example, even if a person's soul is filled with only the material life force, but it is also reflecting a higher-order world, that person might choose teaching as a profession yet aspire to become a holy person. Bapak also pointed to Solomon, who was very rich, to show that the material level also included prophets and religious people.

The Rohani life force of is one order higher than the ordinary human world. Humans cannot enter the world of

Rohani by their own efforts. We can only be lifted into the Rohani world by the grace and help of God. For this to happen, we must give up our self-interest and all interest in this world. In this world, human beings each have their own soul, but in the Rohani world, the human soul is one. Therefore, the worlds beyond the Rohani level are beyond our comprehension; our minds simply cannot imagine them. The human soul is a vessel for the Rohani life force. In other words, the Rohani world is the source of the human soul and its home after death. That is why the Roh Rohani is called the world of "the perfect human being"—the complete form of humankind.

The Great Life Force and the Effects of the Latihan

The Roh Ilofi, or Great Life Force, has special meaning for Subud members because the Latihan comes from this creative force of God. Anyone can join Subud and start to do the Latihan after they are opened.

The Latihan suppresses the working of the mind with a power that is beyond human beings. Just like the horse is bridled and the bull has a nose ring so they can be led quietly to the barn, the consciousness is surrendered so the mind can be led to one side. This creates a spiritual space in the consciousness that is not influenced by the mind. The Great Life Force can then appear, and when it contacts the soul, it flows into the human body through it and starts to purify our whole existence. This occurs in the spiritual world as a result of the Latihan, and that is why the Latihan is a spiritual training without parallel. It is called a training because the process of purification progresses with each Latihan, and members reflect on and make changes in their everyday lives in line with that process. With this purification, the remnants of the desires that lend energy to our minds are gradually cleansed. These remnants consist of unconsumed energy that remains in the form of thoughts, ideas, and emotions attached to our inner selves like stains. Members can measure the progress of their Latihan by how the results of their purification are visibly manifest in their lives.

The purification process starts with the physical body and the senses and then extends to the internal functions of emotion, thought, and consciousness. All parts of our bodies are filled with a spiritual vitality, and our bodies gain spiritual life. This purification continues without compromising our daily lives. It is not like a surgical procedure that requires hospitalization but rather like a prescription for a daily medicine that helps us in our normal lives. The purpose of purification is to wipe away all our dirt so that we can be transformed into a "true human being," but this is a complex process that takes time. Most of the time, we are insensitive to our inner selves and are unaware of the amount of dirt that has accumulated inside of us, including the faults inherited from our parents and ancestors, which are deeply embedded within every part of us. In some cases, this even shapes the character of the person.

We do not yet have the kind of keen, delicate, and purified

sensitivity that would allow us to directly perceive spiritual truth. We can only perceive through the information sent from our coarse sensory organs designed for this material world and transmitted to us as bodily movements. In Latihan, our experience of the spiritual truth is often felt through these bodily movements, which change over time. These movements and utterances occur independently of the will, and they suggest events occurring in the spiritual world. People may laugh without feeling happy or shed tears without feeling sad. Often, they mistake these bodily movements for the substance of Latihan. This is a misunderstanding. Behind the worldly actions of the physical body is the spiritual substance of the soul experiencing contact with the Great Life Force. Laughing without feeling happy is no doubt an expression of the soul's joy in the spiritual world; behind the weeping may be the soul's repentance of their sins against God, in the reality of the next world.

However, even members who have been practicing Latihan for ten or fifteen years find it hard to attain the fine and pure sensitivity needed to directly perceive the realities of the next world. What we do experience is a stillness and peace that arises because the working of the mind has stopped, and worldly thoughts and concerns have disappeared. To be able to go beyond this stage and move to the next takes patience and complete surrender to God. Some people lose patience with this and decide to leave Subud. No one is ever prevented from leaving Subud, and their decision to do so is completely respected.

Only Bapak was capable of sensing what happens in the background of the Latihan. He was the first person to experience Latihan and the only person to experience the full content of the Latihan. When told that the Latihan will purify them, many people think their inner selves are already quite clean. We are insensitive to what is inside our bodies, thinking there is nothing dirty inside us until we excrete it in the form of waste products, and then we do not want to touch it. We wash soil from our clothes and our skin, but we neglect to wash away the bad feelings and thoughts from our minds. These have been gathering inside us since birth, but the problem is that we ourselves are not aware of this.

The function of the Great Life Force is not compatible with the working of the mind, and they cannot coexist; the Great Life Force is not present when the mind is at work. As soon as the mind starts working, it will disappear, and the Latihan will also end. That is the nature of the Latihan—just like elementary particles behave like particles when they are being observed and turn into waves when they are not. Similarly, we can say that the material world, which is the lowest level in the universe, has the dual aspect of both a physical entity and a spiritual entity. The spiritual world instantly becomes a physical one as soon as our minds try to observe it.

Science and Faith

In the previous section, we talked about scientific discoveries of the nineteenth century, dubbed the century of science. During this period, areas of study of the natural world were institutionalized and became divisions of science. There were rapid advancements both qualitatively and quantitatively. At the same time, as knowledge became more and more specialized, it became harder for ordinary people to understand. Technology reinforced the usefulness of scientific discovery, and applied science was born. Lured by the thought that science was a universal panacea that would solve all the mysteries and problems of humankind in the near future, people started to put all their trust in science. With the new arrival of quantum theory in the twentieth century, it is impossible to predict where science will take us in the future.

Despite this exponential growth in science and technology, people have known from the start that the idea of science as a universal panacea was an unsustainable expectation. The methodologies of modern science are fundamentally flawed, as all they have taught us is their application, and all they explain is the reality of a small part of human life. Scientists were aware of this themselves and acknowledged that there was a limit to what science could know. However, they did not actively correct people's belief in science as a universal panacea, and while this belief somewhat lessened over time, people's trust in science is as strong as it ever was. These methodologies cannot be applied to explain psychology and spirituality, and science has never denied their existence. The fact that these methodologies cannot be applied was linked to the theory of materialism, which was no more than a philosophical hypothesis. However, this idea of materialism was taken to be a scientific finding as a result of a scientific inquiry, and it subsequently spread around the world, giving birth to the theory of scientific materialism.

As I mentioned previously, the recent Japanese recipient of the Nobel Prize in Chemistry, Dr. Akira Yoshino, acknowledged that science can explain only 1 or 2 percent of reality. This scientific fact was not commonly shared, and it led to the misconception that nothing exists unless it is recognized by scientific methodology. This led to further confusion, and theories of scientific materialism took hold. That said, it is not my intention to disrespect the achievements of science. I highly appreciate the scientific knowledge of how things in the world work, and I want to make them useful in my life. But at the same time, we cannot ignore the shortcomings of science. Modern science methodologies undermine a holistic understanding of life, and the misunderstandings it has promoted have had a negative impact on humanity.

When the double-slit experiment was conducted and its astonishing results emerged, the experiment had to be repeated several times before the scientists involved would acknowledge the truth of it. Our minds are a function of our brains, but this function has been developed to focus on the material world. So that the mind can fulfil this role efficiently and with minimal effort, it has become blind to the existence of anything that is not of this world. In this way, the mind shows an outstanding ability to recognize the things of the material world, and to understand their mechanisms, but is useless when it comes to perceiving spiritual truths, acting more like a blindfold or sunglasses in the dark. These sunglasses cannot be removed at will like ordinary glasses. They are built into the brain as an integral part of us, and we cannot even remove them when we are sleeping. This aligns with Bapak's assertion that the human mind narrowed its focus over time so that it can concentrate solely on the material things of this world.

CHAPTER 3

THIS WORLD, THE NEXT WORLD, AND THE BARRIER OF DEATH

New Laws for Living

Science eventually revealed that the earth orbits the sun and that dark matter and dark energy exist. This points to the fact that the physical world we know constitutes only a small percentage of the universe. Long before scientific discoveries, the bringer of Christianity, Jesus Christ, was the first to point out that the universe is vast and that the world of heaven (the kingdom of God) is of a different dimension from the material world and is the world that humans should ultimately dwell in. Jesus preached that heaven is near and humans need to repent of their sins. Until then, people knew that heaven existed but saw it as the residence of the gods that had nothing to do with humans. While they also believed that the human soul continues to live after the body has died, they thought that these spirits stayed close to earth, whether it be in the ground under the buried corpse or in the nearby woods and mountains or seas. Jesus told people that heaven was a wonderful place worth any sacrifice, although he did not elaborate on its actual state. Instead, he used parables to explain in much detail the conditions under which we could enter.

One example is the following, described in the Gospel of Matthew when Jesus responds to the belief that people are defiled by what they eat.

> Do you not yet realize that whatever enters the mouth goes into the stomach and then is eliminated? But the things that come out of the mouth come from the heart, and these things defile a man. For out of the heart come evil thoughts, murder, adultery, sexual immorality, theft, false testimony, and slander. These are what defile a man.[3]

These words of Jesus suggest that what pollutes our inner selves are wrong feelings that our minds create. This aligns with Subud's perception of the function of the Latihan, which is to purify ourselves of this dirt—stains that have been accumulating inside us since we were born and that we are not even aware of. The Latihan teaches us our faults and where they have come from. We inherit faults from our parents and ancestors in addition to those we accumulate over our lifetimes.

Some people even embrace these faults and make them an integral part of their own personality.

Jesus added new laws as conditions to entering heaven when he said, "Do not think that I have come to abolish the Law or the Prophets. I have not come to abolish them, but to fulfill them."[4]

Jesus connected humans and our world with heaven, greatly expanding the purpose and the potential of our lives by suggesting we are residents of heaven as well as earth. Jesus was asking people to practice morality while they were living in this world so that they could enter heaven after their death. This created a new standard of conduct for human beings.

Some examples of these are from the Sermon on the Mount of Matthew and the sermons that followed.

Everybody knows the phrase, "Blessed are the poor in spirit for theirs is the kingdom of heaven."[5]

Jesus went on to say this:

> You have heard that it was said to the people long ago, "You shall not murder, and anyone who murders will be subject to judgment." But I tell you that anyone who is angry with a brother or sister will be subject to judgment. Again, anyone who says to a brother or sister, "Raca," is answerable to the court. And anyone who says, "You fool!" will be in danger of the fire of hell.[6]

You have heard that it was said, "You shall not commit adultery." But I tell you that anyone who looks at a woman lustfully has already committed adultery with her in his heart. If your right eye causes you to stumble, gouge it out and throw it away. It is better for you to lose one part of your body than for your whole body to be thrown into hell.[7]

It is as though Jesus is saying that his new commandments and their associated penalties have been passed as laws that are instantly executable even though in this world it is impossible to throw someone into hell. Jesus said this probably because these commandments are the keys to heaven and therefore must be obeyed while we are living in this world. It is too late to do this after our death. The commandments are both for our life in this world and for after our death.

Jesus said that the laws of the land would be completed by the addition of these new rules. These rules were not an attempt to regulate human action in the world but to regulate the mind. The idea of restraining the desires that swirl in the mind was a new morality for humankind. To enter heaven, you must obey that morality. The fundamental differences between us and animals are not physical or functional but rather internal and spiritual and in the way our thoughts and feelings work. Bapak saw Jesus as a role model for humankind.

Bapak's View of Heaven

Just as Jesus was not specific about the state of heaven, Bapak too said little about the higher dimensions beyond the human world—only that it was beyond human imagination. He did remark that everything that exists in this world also exists in the afterworld, but the manner of existence differs greatly between the worlds. There is a separation that exists between the material world and the afterworld that we migrate to after death. This is the reason why we cannot know the state of that world and why death is shrouded in such deep mystery.

Bapak said that people should strive to enter the Rohani world, which is one step higher than the human world. As we saw earlier, the human world is at the center of the cosmic structure, and the human body is material. Bapak explained that it is God's will that humans, whose souls possess the Rohani life force as their content, live in the material world and, when they die, return to the Rohani world, bringing with them the knowledge and experience they gained. This is the real purpose of our lives, he stated.

I cannot think of anyone else who has explained the purpose of life in this way, and no doubt many people would find this hard to accept. However, if it is true, this immediately opens out our field of vision and imparts cosmic meaning to the reason for human existence. It also opens a new understanding of the afterworld. The soul's content is from the Rohani life force, and the knowledge and experience gained through living in this world for a set period provide a highly reliable source of high-quality information that is much more than felt observation. In the Rohani world, where interaction with other worlds is not possible, this is a precious asset.

In his autobiography, Bapak talks about an experience that transcended the separation of life and death. He described this as follows:

> One night, while I was in a state of latihan kejiwaan, there suddenly appeared before me a vast sea with huge waves. Exactly in front of me I saw a dam with a sluice gate that pointed to my mouth. At that instant I moved forward, the sluice gate opened and the water rushed into my open mouth. In a few moments the vast sea was gone and I burped—a sign of being full. The odd thing was that I could smell sea water.[9]

Bapak stopped there and did not go on to explain what this experience signified. Later, he says this:

> In fact I had many experiences of a spiritual nature, but I do not feel it necessary to explain all these here, as otherwise it will only serve to make my children and grandchildren who are

reading this feel bored. I will just relate that
which I feel is important and unusual.[10]

In fact, this was an important and unusual experience.
From other statements of Bapak, we know that this ocean
represents the wall of death that divides this world from the
next. Death is manifested as the ocean to demonstrate the
magnitude of the gap between this world and the next one.
This experience of drinking the ocean of death was followed
by another experience Bapak related.

On this occasion, a book suddenly fell onto his lap. It was
a thick book like a dictionary, but all the pages of the book
were blank. It seemed that if Bapak asked a question of this
strange book, the answer would appear as text on the blank
sheet of paper; if he did not ask a question, the pages would
remain blank. The book eventually disappeared inside Bapak's
chest. After this experience, whenever Bapak had something
he needed to know, he would ask the question of himself, and
immediately he would receive the answer internally.

This is rather different from common spiritual experiences
where the truths or events in the spiritual world we see and
hear are experienced as symbols in this world so that we can
understand them. Sometimes, events in the spiritual world are
mirrored in the material world, but sometimes they do not
become a reality here. Sometimes it may just take some time for
them to be manifest in the world. For example, Bapak was also
given insight into the future and was told there would be a great

war—that Indonesia, which was under Dutch occupation, would become independent and that he himself would travel around the world. It was more than two decades before these events became a reality. During that period, Bapak did know whether or when those changes might happen and why they would eventually lead to a world trip.

Possible reasons for these delays are that the prediction itself is false, or because while events in both worlds resemble each other, their way of manifesting is very different. Whether an event from the other world gets projected into our world or not depends on the circumstances and the location in this world at the time. This world and the next exist side by side but are independent of each other, and for something to happen in this world, it must meet the conditions of this world. Again, ordinary people cannot access the next world unless they cross that great ocean of death. We have no contact with the other world and no way to receive information from it. Our minds are designed to understand only the things in this world. We were created so that our minds would not focus on anything other than the world we live in.

The Latihan is a blessing from God that was given to us so that we can suppress the working of the mind and contact the spiritual world without the interference of the mind. In Latihan, it becomes harder to think and feel because we are in contact with the spiritual world. In this state, the mind is not put to sleep but simply set aside, and at any time, the attention can be directed to the mind's workings. At that moment, the Latihan will finish, and the person returns to their normal self.

The experiences Bapak had of drinking up the ocean and of the mysterious blank book that gave him instant answers to his questions in real life were, in this way, far removed from the ordinary. What happened at that time was that inside Bapak, the barrier of death was crossed, connecting this world with the next as if they were adjoining countries, so that God's will in the other world was carried out directly in this world. The limitations of this world were disregarded, and the result was a miracle. Bapak talked about how answers were written on the blank pages of the book, which meant he would receive the answers internally. What occurred in the next world became real in this world through Bapak's experience of it.

What Are Miracles?

Until Bapak's first visit to the UK in 1957, Subud was completely unknown in the West. No one had heard of it, and because Bapak was Indonesian, he was often misunderstood or treated with prejudice. Unexpectedly, however, the miraculous healing from ovarian cancer of a British-Hungarian film actress who had joined Subud and went on to give birth became widespread news. Through some unexpected connections with a Gurdjieff group, this news spread around the UK as well as the rest of Europe. This was really a miracle that was in accordance with

God's will, as over two or three years, Subud grew rapidly in dozens of countries and regions and spread to all five continents.

In my opinion, this is similar to when Jesus performed the miracles described in the Bible. According to the Bible, Jesus walked on water, instantly healed many people with incurable diseases, resurrected a dead disciple, and satisfied the hunger of thousands of people with a few loaves of bread. In the end, he was sentenced to death, but three days later, he returned from the dead and appeared in front of his disciples. None of these events can be explained by science, and scientists dismiss them as religious myth. However, if, as Jesus thought, this world and the spiritual world are one and not separate, these sorts of miracles are not an anomaly. If there is no distinction between this world and the next, the truth of the spiritual world becomes the truth of this world; and if an inhabitant of heaven comes down to this world to allow humans to live in heaven (God's kingdom), the relationship between heaven and earth are made apparent in the life he leads. God's will in heaven becomes God's will on earth as manifest through His actions.

It is also the case that some people, even if they are not special beings like Jesus, experience a miracle or something close to a miracle. It is beyond my scope to understand this, but my guess is that at the time, that person's mind was not filled with the issues of this world, and they were in a state close to relinquishing all worldly interest. The interests of this world are assets that enrich the mind, and giving them up impoverishes the mind. It is symbolic that the Virgin Mary only appeared to children in Lourdes and other places. Jesus said we cannot enter the kingdom of heaven unless we become like a child, that it is impossible to serve both riches and God, and that it is easier for a camel to pass through the eye of a needle than for a rich person to enter heaven. Whether a person's mind is rich or poor depends on whether it is filled with the thoughts and knowledge of the world. The mind of an adult is filled with these things, but the minds of newborns are not. Their minds can function, yet there is no content: their minds are poor. From the moment of birth, the baby starts to accrue knowledge of this world, gradually increasing the content of its mind as it grows. The accumulation of knowledge of this world becomes its mind's assets (wealth). The baby grows into an adult and, as a result, loses contact with its soul. This is possibly what the words of Jesus refer to here.

As I mentioned, I imagine that miracles appear to adults whose minds are free of worldly interests and who are resigned in themselves. This creates a kind of poverty of the mind that brings them closer to heaven and puts them in a state where it is probably more likely that miracles can occur. There is something else about this state and the Latihan I would like to add here. In the Latihan of Subud, the working of the mind is suppressed, which then creates a space in which the mind is emptied—its content impoverished. The mind stops working, and as soon as it starts to work again, the Latihan stops. This is the case for most members in Subud. However, there is potential beyond this, as exemplified by Bapak, in whom the working of the Latihan was truly compatible with the working of his mind. This is a state whereby the Latihan continued within him while at the same time he functioned like everyone else in normal life, using his mind to think and his heart to feel. Someone who has attained this state will always be protected and guided by God, even as they use their mind to fulfill the daily needs of this world as normal. The person will feel this for themselves. Bapak jokingly said that this was like someone repeating, *God! God!* as they counted banknotes, while their Latihan continued inside them.

Bapak also said the Latihan was *hakekat*—a way to experience spiritual reality—while the final stage where there is a balance between the Latihan and the working of the mind was *Marifat*, which is the ultimate goal and destination of someone in Subud. Marifat is not easy to attain. It can remain a distant ideal even for someone who has been doing Latihan all their life. That is why people say it is easy to do Latihan but hard to attain this stage. As a member of Subud who spent time close to Bapak, I was able to witness the reality of Marifat through his experience. He also said that Marifat was the state of the prophets and that the goal of Subud was to foster the growth of people who could be in this state. This subject, however, is beyond our comprehension, and so I will leave it at that.

Bapak's Ascension Experience

As mentioned earlier, Bapak explained that the universe consists of seven different types of life forces, which are independent and autonomous entities. They cannot interact with or have free access to one another. To compensate for this, the Great Life Force creates a passageway that penetrates to the depths of all the forces and provides a way for each force to move one step up to the next level. This is like a stairway to heaven.

Humans hold a special place in the universe. While our souls have a content that is higher than the human life force and that represents our true selves, our bodies are made of matter and can live in the material world on earth. Humans can coexist with the material, vegetable, and animal forces in this world and be aware of their state. However, we cannot go to higher-order realms beyond the human, and we cannot have knowledge of them. Bapak's ascension experience, therefore, has significance for us and is a precious legacy that must not be forgotten.

Bapak reports this experience in his autobiography but in a brief description. He tells us that he will only describe things that he himself has experienced directly, and as such, this is a valuable source of information for us. The following is a summary of some of the most important aspects of the story.

When he was a boy, Bapak once had a strange dream in which he was told by a man dressed in black that he would be called to God at the age of thirty-two. He assumed that being called to God meant to die. In fact, when he was thirty-two, what really happened was not death but a call from God to travel the heavens. In his ascension experience, Bapak left the earth and the solar system and travelled beyond the galactic universe, passing through the seven conical heavens, until he reached the seventh and highest heaven.

The first thing he experienced was that his body started to expand until it had enveloped the entire planet. That expanded body then broke apart, and Bapak was launched into the void at a furious speed. He passed through the sun to the other side of the solar system. He said he did this not by orbiting the sun and exiting the solar system but by passing through a tunnel inside the sun to get to the outer world. While Bapak did not specify this, it is assumed that this tunnel in the sun is in fact the passageway created by the Great Life Force. Oddly, while passing through the sun, he felt nothing of its heat and glare. Then, before he knew it, his body had transformed into the same light substance as the sun.

As mentioned, each level of the universe is a living entity with its own conditions, created by a different life force. To be able to access any of these levels, or worlds, you must have a body that meets the conditions of that world. In Bapak's case, this transformation happened automatically. When Bapak left the solar system, he could see far in the distance something that sparkled like diamonds. When he asked what it was, he was told it was the galactic universe that he had just left. As he flew on at an accelerating speed, at the ends of the void, he could see seven cone-shaped objects that were piled on top of each other. This was the seven-layered heaven. When he entered the first cone, he found himself in a mysterious space whose interior seemed larger than its exterior. He then started to gradually ascend from the bottom layer up, through a passageway that connected all seven cones. He felt himself start to lose power. When he was raised up to the seventh cone, all power was taken from him, and all he could do was chant, "Allah! Allah! Allah!" In that cone-shaped space, there was no direction and no purpose. However, he was able to see things that were way in the distance as clearly as though they were in front of his eyes. For example, he could clearly see his eldest son sleeping halfway out of his bed at home on the other side of the universe.

Through this ascension experience, Bapak was able to confirm the reality of the spiritual universe with his own eyes.

What Kind of World Is the Afterlife?

Death is the greatest mystery we face. Death is pivotal to our understanding of what it is to be human. Life and death are two sides of the same whole; if we understand what life is and what it means to live, we might understand what death is and what happens at death. Science has no answers, and because it does not know the fundamental purpose of our existence, it does not address the issue.

Science cannot even determine the moment a person dies. Of course, when a person dies, a doctor must declare the death, and this has resulted in much discussion over how to define death. The general definition of death was accepted as a lack of pulse, the absence of breathing, and the dilation of the pupils. However, with the advent of organ transplantation, it became clear that this alone was not sufficient to declare the person dead, and this standard definition was abandoned. These days, the more accepted theory is to determine the point of death as the moment the brain dies. However, this too is not without controversy. There are hundreds of millions of cells in the brain, and it is scientifically impossible to tell which cells ceased functioning and at what point. Even if you define death as the moment when all the brain cells stop working, it is impossible to pinpoint the moment in which this happened.

Death is an intimate and hugely significant part of our lives. No one can escape it. We will all die someday; at its longest, life expectancy is around 120 years old. We all want to understand what happens to us when we die. Will it be painful? Is there life after death? We are separated from death by a thick wall, and once we die, we can never return to this world. No one has come back to tell us about the state of death or the afterlife, and we cannot expect this to ever happen. This why people fear death. Death is an unknown darkness. We want to escape from this unknown place where our experiences in this world serve no purpose. We live life avoiding the subject of death and doing our best not to think about it or even let it enter our consciousness.

For hardcore materialists, it is a straightforward matter:

human beings are physical bodies that, when they die, decompose and are reduced to chemical elements that return to earth or float in the atmosphere. Materialism denies the existence of God, the spirit, and the soul as well as all spiritual and religious experiences, which are considered delusional. To materialists, when the human body dies, neither the self nor the consciousness exists. All that is left is an imaginary consciousness that is a construct of the brain. Since materialism is supported by modern science, many people today are aligned with this way of thinking. However, recently, many people have come to hold a different view. In Japan, for example, it seems that more and more people now visit shrines on New Year's Day or visit their family's graves on the anniversary of their death. Religious festivals are also becoming more popular year by year. Buoyed by ancient human intuition, these people believe that the soul will continue to live after the body has died. They do not doubt that the consciousness of the self and the thoughts and emotions that it comprises will continue to live on in the afterlife, even after the death of the physical body. Thoughts and emotions are not solid matter, and therefore it cannot be scientifically proven that they die with the physical death of the body.

In Bapak's view, humans' consciousness of self, their thoughts, and emotions are not substantial matter, so when the physical body dies, these are transported to the afterlife. However, as death heralds the end of the physical body that created these activities and supplied them with energy, these same activities cannot continue after death. What survives is only the thoughts and feelings produced just before death, but these cannot be amended, nor can new content be added to them. Therefore, many people believe that it is impossible to lie if you are questioned in the afterlife. This also gives rise to the belief that even many years after their death, there are dead people who think that they are not yet dead and continue to have the thoughts and consciousness that they had just before death. To change this situation, we need to replace the physical body that functions in this world with a spiritual body that has awareness in the world of the afterlife. Spiritualism and theology have long pointed out that we are not supplied with spiritual bodies from the outset, but rather we must create them through right living in this world. This was a perception that Bapak newly brought to the world.

The Institute of Statistical Mathematics, an external organization of Japan's Ministry of Education, Culture, Sports, Science, and Technology, conducts awareness surveys every year in conjunction with other countries. Results from these suggest that while many Japanese people are skeptical of religion, they show a similar amount of religious feeling to people in other countries and express a particularly high level of interest in reincarnation. Since we cannot directly know the existence or absence of an afterlife, we seek indirect ways to guess at this. From long ago, people sought to interact with the afterlife—for example, God, spirits, and dead souls—through fortune-tellers or the mediation of mediums and psychics. These attempts are continued by spiritualists, and many books provide information about the afterlife obtained through interaction with the spirits of the dead.

These days, we have increased access to reports of near-death and out-of-body experiences. While these reports may invite skepticism, the uniformity of the information they provide suggests a high level of reliability. We cannot obtain direct evidence of the afterlife, and so, to some extent, we must rely on these indirect experiences. This is somewhat like a court trial, where there is no direct evidence available, such as fingerprints or DNA testing or confession, and the truth is determined by gathering indirect evidence. Historically, all over the world, spiritual mediums, shamans, and psychics allow themselves to be possessed by the spirits of the gods or dead people so that they can communicate through them. This was initially used by rulers and kings for political purposes, such as predicting good fortune, but gradually its use was expanded to meet the needs of ordinary people. In this way, people also started to become mediums as a profession and are still active today.

The View of the Spiritualists

In Europe, séances boomed in the second half of the eighteenth century, and famous writers and scholars often took part. Spiritualist movements continue this tradition. The International Council of Spiritualists, for example, has adopted the following seven principles based on records and testimonies of spiritual movements over more than two centuries.

1. The fatherhood of God
2. The brotherhood of man
3. Communication between incarnate and discarnate spirit
4. The continuation of individual life with its own characteristics after bodily death
5. Personal responsibility
6. Compensation or retribution here or hereafter for all deeds done on earth
7. A path of eternal progress open to every spirit

The third principle, *Communication between incarnate and discarnate spirit*, reflects a growing tendency to take into account the involvement of spirits, while the seventh one, *A path of eternal progress open to every spirit*, is a clear denial of the idea that once we go to hell, the path of salvation will be closed.

The world of the afterlife, as envisioned by spiritualists, is connected to this world through a progression of waveforms that gradually transform from coarse to fine until they become the most delicate waveforms closest to God—like a piece of fabric where intense colors at one end gradually blur into softer shades at the other end. After death, the soul ascends to the infinite expansion of the other world, its waveforms matching the stage it is at, and "the path of eternal progress" is opened to them.

It is strange that none of these seven principles mention reincarnation, and this could be because there is a conflict of opinion among well-known psychics as to whether reincarnation exists or not, and no agreement can be reached on the matter. Neither orthodox Christianity nor Islam allow for reincarnation. Both systems believe that after death, humans sleep underground until the day of the last judgment.

Although Bapak was Muslim, he recognized reincarnation. He often referred to life after death, but he never spoke systematically about what we will experience after we die or what kind of life the soul lives in the other world. When asked about the meaning of death by Subud member Varindra Vittachi, Bapak refrained from explaining this, saying that we were not yet ready to face the truth of death. He did go on to describe the three possible destinations after death as a rough and interim answer. This was described in detail in my previous book (*Latihan—A Path to the Great Life and a New Way to Purify the Soul*, pp. 81–82), but because of its significance, I will explain it again here with an introduction to Varindra.

Varindra Tarzie Vittachi was a world-class journalist who had close relationships with several political leaders. He was critical of the dictatorship in Sri Lanka (then Ceylon) and won the Magsaysay Prize in 1959 for his book about the government's involvement in the country's race riots. This led him to be declared persona non grata by the state. He later moved to the United States, became a regular columnist of *Newsweek* magazine, and served as an executive of UNICEF. He also served for many years as the head of Subud's international organization. While he worked for Subud, he never disclosed his membership on account of his social position. I was his good friend, and in later years, he told me he was going to declare this. However, he died before he could do so.

In response to Varindra's question about death, Bapak said that there were too many possibilities to talk generally about, but as a provisional answer, however, he offered the following explanation as to the three potential destinations after we die. 1) Many people in the modern world have materialistic thoughts and feelings that they wear like armor. After they die, this pulls them deep into the bottom of the material world. 2) Then there are those who are less materialistic but still cannot escape the material world, and so they remain here after death. Their only choice is to be reborn as a human so that they get another chance through another existence. 3) Finally, a very small number of people are raised to heaven as soon as they die.

If you read the testimonies of people who have had near-death or out-of-body experiences, it is clear that they witnessed a world of space and time not of this world, even though this may not represent the world after death. There is no spatial distance there as there is in this world. If you want to go somewhere, you are instantly there. Some people have even spoken about going back in time and encountering head-on something that happened in the past. If they did have glimpses of the afterlife in that critical near-death or out-of-body state, they would have temporarily penetrated the thick wall that separates us from death. No one can be sure of any this, however, and reading Bapak's various explanations and leaving aside people with near-death experiences, questions remain as to whether the world glimpsed by people with out-of-body experiences is an illusion created by their minds.

Testing in Subud

Spiritualism states that there is communication between the incarnate and discarnate spirit but does not fully explain what this communication involves. Bapak described this relationship, saying that everything that exists in this world also exists in the afterlife but in a different form. He encouraged Subud members to try to experience this relationship for themselves through a kind of Latihan called testing.

Every member of Subud has the potential to receive spiritual experiences. Through the Latihan, we have an opportunity to witness spiritual truths. Whether we receive this opportunity or not depends on God's will. This kind of experience is not had simply by wanting it; nor is it something you can always avoid, nor something you need qualifications for. Spiritual experiences arrive suddenly and without notice, regardless of whether you are prepared or not. Some people are given these experiences not long after they have started doing Latihan, and some even have them in their opening (first) Latihan.

In most cases, the experiencing of a spiritual truth is a blessing. It deepens your faith in God and strengthens your confidence in Subud. However, it brings with it a certain responsibility, as you are now a witness to that spiritual truth. Bapak often used testing to help members struggling with Latihan to experience spiritual truth. Testing is a form of Latihan where a member quietens all thoughts in complete surrender to God, asks the question they need to understand, and then starts their Latihan. During this Latihan, they receive an answer, and how they receive that answer depends on the extent of their purification. For example, if their purification is only at the corporeal level, they will receive the answer as bodily movements. One way this might happen could be if moved by the power of the Latihan, you find you are shaking your head from side to side regardless of your will, suggesting a negative answer. On the other hand, a vertical nod of your head suggests a positive answer. Some people receive the answer as an inner feeling, some see it as a visual image, and some people find their lips moving and words emerging unbidden. The way each person receives these answers depends on how far, how deep, and in which parts of their body this purification has progressed. How this process is possible is a mystery, but it is experienced by every member in Subud.

These test questions must be of a spiritual content. Our mind and our feelings are used to solve worldly problems, and that is their purpose. In cases where the issue is a material one, but it has an impact on someone's whole life, then it can be also be tested. While spiritual experiences and tests both symbolically show spiritual truths, they are not the same. That is why the person often does not understand the nature of the truth they have been shown. Often, however, if they leave it aside, they find that understanding comes to them later through an event they experience. Sometimes they do not receive an answer, and that too is acceptable. Perhaps that person has not reached the right state to receive that answer or does not need to know it yet. We who live in this world cannot know—nor do we need to know—everything that occurs or does not occur in the spiritual world. All members are given the opportunity to experience spiritual truth for themselves through the means of testing.

The Jupiter Test

Bapak once conducted a test in Japan about the planet Jupiter that made a strong and lasting impression on me. In that test, Bapak first asked members to receive in their Latihan an answer to the question, "How big are potatoes on Jupiter?" Some members received "very big," so then Bapak asked, "What kind of hearts do the inhabitants or beings of Jupiter possess?" This was a new and unusual question for us to test. Normally, it is beyond our capabilities to understand worlds other than the earth, and we could not do so without Bapak's help, so he rarely made it the subject of a test.

At that time, I was sitting side by side with Bapak, as

my role was to interpret into Japanese from English, which was being interpreted from Bapak's Indonesian speech. I had no intention to participate in the test, as I was focused on interpreting. However, because it was a very unusual question, I hurriedly interpreted it into Japanese and then tried to receive the answer in a Latihan state like the rest of the members. In the next instant, I experienced something incredible. A silvery-white mist seemed to gush out from my heart, shining and spreading out in front of me. This lasted no more than a few seconds, but it showed me that Jupiter's inhabitants are on a much higher level than humans, and rather than leak emotions, their hearts glow and shine with a delicate, translucent mist.

Previously, I had heard Bapak say that there are inhabitants in every celestial body, and some are of a higher level than humans, while some are lower. The conditions of these celestial bodies are very different from those on earth, so of course, we would need space suits to visit and interact directly with their inhabitants. However, he said, it was possible to interact with them on a spiritual level. This test about Jupiter gave me a concrete understanding of what this meant.

My Experience of the Passageway to Heaven

The following story was a spiritual experience I once had during a group Latihan.

At that time, Subud Japan rented a large sports hall from a high school for our Latihans. The hall had no heating, and the wind blew in through gaps in the window and doorframes, so in winter I would wear a coat while doing Latihan. One night, shortly after I had started Latihan, I noticed that I seemed to be standing inside a transparent cylindrical tube. I looked up, and it seemed as though the cylinder was extending directly upward, as though to the very ends of the infinite heavens. It vaguely occurred to me that somewhere at the end of the tube was the throne of God. I was confused. How was it that I could see to the ends of heaven? I looked around, and the inside walls of the cylindrical tube appeared to be pitch-black. When I looked through the transparent wall of the cylinder, the outside world was a little brighter because of the fine dust floating in the atmosphere that was reflecting light. Then I realized that the reason I could see the end of the cylinder was that there were absolutely no impurities or dust inside it, and that was possibly why it was so dark there.

When I looked up through the cylinder again to check, I saw that it had no distortions or bends in it but stretched up perfectly straight. All the while, my Latihan continued as usual. I felt sad that I was standing on the floor at the very bottom of the cylinder. After a few years of Latihan, I had expected to be floating at least two or three meters above the floor by then. Fortunately, that thought soon disappeared. Even if I were to float hundreds of meters above ground, it would make no difference, considering the distance from God, who is infinitely far but also infinitely close.

I learned by this experience that the important thing for

us is not to judge our progress or how high we think we are but rather to just keep walking ahead without stopping. We have already been given a passageway to God. Since there are no obstacles in this passageway, there is no need to step into a side street of self-appraisal. Even if you think it is a shortcut, it will turn into the long way around, and you could end up losing your way and losing sight of the passageway itself. This was reinforcement for a similar experience I had had in my prior Latihan.

In that Latihan, a wall of light suddenly appeared on the floor of the sports hall. This wall of light penetrated up through the ceiling and pushed down through the tatami mats on the floor, with small bubbles of light appearing where it made contact with these. Since the wall was around ten meters thick, I thought it was a wall of light, but then for some reason, it occurred to me that it was God's foot. However, to assume that God has feet is to anthropomorphize a supreme being and is ordinarily unacceptable. Even in Latihan, I had that much sense. Nevertheless, the thought became so strong it was hard to deny. The group Latihan finished then, ending this experience without any understanding of it. However, when I experienced the cylindrical passageway in the following Latihan, I realized that the view of the wall of light was the view of the cylinder from the outside. It was the outside and inside of the same thing. That was why I thought the wall of light was God's foot.

When I reflect on this now, I think that the cylinder was a

symbol of the Latihan. I was made to experience the spiritual essence of the Latihan, which cannot be understood through words, in a symbolic way that was easier to understand. This kind of spiritual experience is characteristic of Subud, and it is of much interest to me.

My Mother's Death and the Latihan

I spoke about most of my experiences with death in my first book, *Subud—A Spiritual Journey* (2008). From those experiences, I learned that there are many kinds of death and that when some people die, it takes them a while to realize that they are dead. In that book, I did not talk about the following experience related to my mother's passing.

My mother was opened in Subud while I was still young. As I mentioned in my earlier book, she was not able to do Latihan for various reasons, either with a group or by herself. When she was elderly, she chose to enter a nursing home in the country, which was about an hour's train ride away from Kisarazu, Chiba, where I was living. This meant that my wife and I were only able to visit her occasionally, and she did not have much opportunity to do Latihan. She died at the age of eighty-six, after which I experienced a lingering regret.

One of the core beliefs of Subud is that the benefits of our doing the Latihan extend not only to us but also to our parents and even family members who have already died. I had already experienced this while my father was dying a painful death at a young age. At that time, I was given unexpected contact with him through the Latihan, which offered him relief from his condition. On the other hand, when my mother died, absolutely nothing seemed to have changed. A few days after her death, I joined the group Latihan. As soon I started, I noticed that the content of my Latihan was different from usual.

In the next moment, I had the realization that my mother's soul was inside my chest and that she was doing Latihan with me. This feeling was strong and alive, and there was no mistaking what it was. As soon as my Latihan finished, the feeling subsided. This experience unexpectedly lasted for nearly three months. Every time I did my Latihan, I was aware that my mother's soul was doing Latihan together with me. Although she had not been able to do enough Latihan while she was alive, for those months, she stayed inside me and made up for this lack.

I had never thought such a thing could be possible—particularly because Subud does not allow for men and women to do Latihan together. Wives and husbands, parents and children of the opposite sex always do Latihan separately. People often question why this is the case, but there is a clear reason: when we do Latihan, our natures and the state of our inner selves are exposed. Normally, our inner selves are concealed behind the mask of our persona—the personality that is created by the working of our mind. In Latihan, this working of the mind is suppressed by the power of God, and our hidden inner selves and our character come to the surface. These are manifested by the sounds and movements our bodies make in Latihan. For example, a man might shout in Latihan, or a woman might cry out; these sounds are part of their process of purification that is set in motion by the Latihan. The energy that produced the current state of their inner selves burns up and disappears. However, if men and women do Latihan together, the potential for them to receive the Latihan that is right for them diminishes, as they are conscious of the behavior of the opposite sex. Moreover, there is a greater possibility for misunderstandings to arise, creating problems between men and women. For these reasons, the general rule is that men and women do Latihan separately.

During Latihan, there is always awareness. People do not enter a trancelike state; they are always conscious of what they are doing. However, our spiritual experience in Subud often involves a sense of reality that is much more intense than what we experience in our daily lives. This strong sense of reality allows Subud members to be convinced of the truthfulness of these experiences; however, if we are not attentive, we risk confusing truth in the spiritual realm with truth in this world. We make the mistake of thinking that whatever happens in the spiritual realm also happens in this world. The spiritual world must not be confused with this world; events that occur in one are not mirrored in the other. The fact is that these two worlds have different conditions and different realities. Any actions that disregard this difference will disrupt the order of this world. Bapak himself told me to pay attention to this.

Even if you know that something is occurring in the other world through your spiritual experience, it will not happen in this world unless the right conditions are in place, or it might take some time, as I mentioned earlier. If it turns out that this event does not take place in this world, no matter; it just means that the relevance it had to this world has ceased to be, and therefore you should forget about it. Bapak advised members who had experienced something in their Latihan not to believe in it until it became a reality in this world. It is a delicate issue, but I remember Bapak saying that while the things of this world do exist in the other world, their manner of existence differs.

CHAPTER 4

IN SEARCH OF A
GRAND DESIGN

Key Preoccupations of Our Age

Associate Professor Naoki Kashio specializes in religious studies
at the Faculty of Letters, Keio University, a well-known private
university in Japan. In his book, *Spirituality Revolution*,[11]
Kashio provides a detailed analysis of contemporary religion
and identifies anxiety and loneliness as keywords of our age.
Today, our world is characterized by a globalism brought
about by an internet-centered information revolution that has
shattered the barriers of distance around the world. This was
also aided by the growth of airline networks making world
travel easily accessible. The world became integrated faster than
anyone expected. Communication with friends and family on
the other side of the world and video access is available in an
instant and at little cost.

This globalization is a positive factor economically, as
it promotes the distribution and trade of goods and opens

business opportunities. Ease of communication with people and countries around the world also expands areas of cooperation. However, there are downsides to this. As the world became connected, every culture on the earth became only as good as the next culture. People started to compare cultures and incorporate other cultures to replace their own, but criticism of this phenomenon was condemned. This situation has only intensified, affecting people in every corner of the globe. Until now, people acquired their standards of conduct based on the traditional culture they were raised in and gave these absolute values. They relied on this judgment in their everyday lives. However, in a world where everything is relativized, it may be possible to compare good and evil, but none of it is absolute. There is not absolute truth; everything is uncertain.

All nations are connected to one another, and so what happens in some country today may happen in your country tomorrow, and you can no longer be sure of what might happen to your own self in the future. Interestingly, this corresponds to facts revealed by science in the uncertainty principle. An important fundamental principle of quantum mechanics, the uncertainty principle states that measurements of elementary particles inherently involve uncertainty; the more precise the measurement, the more disruption to the measurement itself. In the same way, if there is nothing certain in this world, everyone who has based their standards of conduct on the value of their traditional culture loses that reliable source. Nothing can truly be relied on.

The connections between people are through shared bloodlines or culture. However, even these relationships lose certainty and are diluted by this loss of absolute values. It becomes less certain that we can rely on our family, relatives, or friends in an emergency. The result is inevitably that people become self-centered and individualism prevails, giving precedence to convenience and profit. However, individualism leads to loneliness and anxiety. If people only rely on themselves, the relationship with society is lost, giving rise to this sense of isolation. Uncertainty about the future creates a sense of anxiety. Humans were not made to live apart from society. Some organisms do live alone except for when they reproduce, but humans cannot live that way. Humans are dependent on one another. Babies would not survive without being cared for.

This material world is full of harsh challenges for all living things. The socially vulnerable and the elderly cannot survive without the care of others. While governments need to strengthen their welfare policies and address this issue, they face many challenges. Welfare is expensive, and too much welfare dampens the economy, so it is hard to get the entire nation on board with these policies. To overcome this, the spirit of helping one another needs to be embedded in society as a whole. It is not easy to divest people of their fundamental self-interest in a world where the fittest survive and transform them into people who value a society of mutual help. The mind is governed by the law of inertia, which acts like a force to keep things as they are rather than being open to change.

According to Bapak, human desires increased dramatically during a period of history that coincided with the appearance of Jesus Christ. Bapak did not clearly state that this was a causal relationship, but the appearance of Jesus was possibly God's way of controlling the confusion caused by these increased desires of humankind; indeed, the reining in of desires was core to Jesus's teachings.

The ideal of a unified world has been a dream of humanity for many years, and bringing the world together was seen as the only way to eradicate the endless wars waged since history began. Both the United Nations and the European Union (EU) were created for that purpose. However, with the United States and China currently fighting for domination and Brexit in the UK a real possibility, we seem to be heading in the opposite direction.

I imagine the state of the world now as a great ocean of human desire in which everyone sails around aimlessly, either in their own small boat of desire or in a bigger passenger boat. The waves created by the bows of the little boats are the desires of those inside them. These waves crash toward and away from one another, colliding and growing and creating vortexes. These vortexes grow into massive whirlpools that can result in conflict and war.

Rozak Tatebe

The Solace of Religion

When humans were lost as to how to deal with natural and man-made disasters in this world, religion appeared in order to guide and counsel them. I have already described the struggle for supremacy at Galileo's trial in the seventeenth century when Christian theologians insisted on the bible-based Ptolemaic theory of the universe, and scientists advocated the Copernican theory of observation and experimentation. Although the theologians won the trial at the time, science ultimately triumphed. Religion then began to lose authority and has never been able to recover it. Moreover, there does not seem to be a way for trust in religion to be restored. One of the reasons for this is the growing secularity of religious people themselves because of the many benefits that science offers. Psychologists and psychoanalysts have become the counsellors of the people rather than clergymen.

Associate Professor Kashio also noted that the word *spirituality* is now more often used around the world to represent the sense of religion inherent in everyone, rather than institutionalized religion. The notion of spirituality is becoming more and more common in wider areas of society. He suggests that this is not a temporary phenomenon but rather a strategy that humanity has unconsciously chosen in response to the anxiety and loneliness of society today. Kashio expresses his hope that this trend will give birth to a new, high-order spirituality that will lead to a more open religion of deeper content and the potential for high self-transcendence. He goes on to say that an open religion is essentially a religious attempt to solve loneliness, the root of many of the world's problems. It is the only way the self can become conscious of the fact that we are not alone and that we have always been one, thus reviving our consciousness from before we became human beings. Religions have historically offered cultural resources for individuals to reach that level of transcendence, and to do this now, they need to become more open.

To support this conclusion, Kashio examines and analyzes a wide range of new religious cultures, therapies, and popular cultures. I will not describe these here but will say that the Latihan of Subud, which I have practiced for many years, offers a close match to the conditions of the open religion Kashio describes. I list these conditions below:

- Its primary objective is the search for the principles of spirituality through awareness of spiritual states (union with absolute being).
- It respects the independence and will of the individual.
- The purpose of the community is not to expand the size of the group or the size of its facilities.
- Joining and leaving are relatively free.
- It does not proselytize as a means of deepening faith.
- It is not attached to gurus or sacred places and myths associated with them.

- It does not make its leader a living god, nor create hierarchies.
- Rituals and practices are aimed at exploring spiritual principles.
- It eliminates bureaucracy.
- It offers plentiful volunteer services inside and outside the group.
- Donations are freely given.
- There is open dialogue and inquiry; nothing is secret.
- It allows expression of beliefs in one's own self-transcendental consciousness.

Latihan and the organization of Subud meet most of these conditions, and that is the reason I suggest that Bapak's perceptions of the cosmos and humanity be used as a grand design for humanity today.

The Longing for Freedom

Everyone longs for freedom, regardless of who they are—from students to politicians. Some people can sense that the world we live in is not the entire universe and there is a world of greater and more expansive freedom above our skies. Often, such people are highly creative and feel a sense of joy and purpose when they experience this for themselves. They are instinctively uncomfortable in this world and constantly seek out other worlds of higher quality.

I once talked to a famous songwriter who described the

creation of her best lyrics as words delivered from heaven. At such moments, she felt elevated beyond the reality of this world, full of the joy and satisfaction of her work. Music is probably one of the best ways to feel transported beyond this world. Literature and the visual arts start from the reality of this world, which we see and hear with our eyes and ears, but music starts from a place beyond the things of the world, and its beauty is capable of reaching people around the world. World-famous conductor Bruno Walter once said that, with a few exceptions, the music you hear is not musical creation so much as the vibrations of another cosmic world expressed as music that is felt by our inner ear, which is the organ of our soul. In his book, *Time with the Oboe*, well-known Japanese oboe player Fumiki Miyamoto said this:

> When I'm blowing the oboe, I don't feel my own weight—the power of the music creates a virtual reality paradise. It is the nature of the performer to want to embody this special moment.
>
> You play an instrument to become free … you become the sound itself and fly around in the air. You cling to nothing; you are completely free.[12]

Miyamoto is saying that the performer's ultimate goal is to go beyond themselves, and by doing so to transcend the world with greater freedom.

Art is the act of creating a beauty that does not yet exist in the world. It is about expressing and expanding the self. The moment of creation is a moment of transcendence of the self that experiences a freer world. This is probably why artists make so many sacrifices to devote their lives to art. It is also the case for athletes. When asked why he was climbing a mountain, one world-class climber said, "Because the mountain was there!" This non-answer does not mean much, but it does reflect a yearning for greater freedom.

A Conversation between God and the Angels on Human Creation

Regarding the freedoms given to humans, Bapak told members a fascinating story from the scriptures about a conversation between God and angels on the goal of human creation.

After God created the universe, He said that He wanted to gather the angels and see with His own eyes the universe He had created. Angels are the servants of God, and they are made of light. People usually want to see for themselves the result of their creations, so it is easy to understand why God also had such a thought. God wanted to see the results of His creation with His own eyes. He also wanted to check this through the eyes of a third party—namely the angels, who He sent into space. Angels can travel a thousand times faster than light, but the universe God created was so vast it took a hundred years for them reach the edge of the universe and return to Him.

God told the angels He had created the universe as a vessel, and therefore it needed inhabitants, and so He created these. Regarding the creation of human beings, He told them that they would not be like the angels, made of light, but that they would return to Him like them or maybe even sooner than them. The angels were shocked and speechless at this because even angels who travel faster than light take a hundred years to get to the end of the universe and back. Based on this understanding, it should take humans seventy million years to reach God. However, God replied, 'This is My will. I am almighty." To make this happen, He said He would bury the essence of God inside each creation. The angels were persuaded when they heard Him say this and promised to obey God's will.

This is a synopsis of the story. Bapak pointed out that three days after his crucifixion, Jesus Christ ascended to heaven, the prophet Muhammad ascended in a day, and Bapak's experience of ascension also took seven hours. What this conversation between God and the angels also implies is that human beings have an important role in the universe—that of inspecting and reporting on the universe in the same way as the angels do. A human being can return to God faster than an angel. The human world is located at the center of the universe, and inside the human soul is a life force that is higher than the human world. However, as we know, the body is made of matter so it can inhabit the material world of the earth. The idea that God intended us to return to the Rohani world with the knowledge and experience gained in this world is reflected in this conversation between God and angels.

Free Will and Religion

What is unique to humans is that in this world, we can exercise a free will that is close to God's. We can judge right or wrong instead of God and act freely based on our judgment. The result can be of great benefit or of absolute disaster to the world. In the cosmic order, the higher the world, the less it is bound by laws and the greater the degree of freedom. Matter cannot move by itself; plants cannot walk around, but they are given the freedom to extend their roots into the earth and stretch toward the sun; animals can freely move around and expand the world they live in. Human beings have an even greater degree of freedom, but it does not meet our standards when you consider our cosmic origins.

Humans always dreamed of flight, and Leonardo Da Vinci designed the first flying contraption in human history. It took another four hundred years before the dream was realized by the Wright brothers. This dream of flying through the skies did not end there. We built jets, launched rockets, and now we target the space beyond our solar system. We spare no effort to make our dreams come true, to overcome our individual limitations and those of all humankind. The struggle to attain a freer world never ends.

Animal and other subhuman organisms also desire freedom. To have desire is to be alive and is a necessity that cannot be eliminated but only limited. In animals, actions based on desire are limited by instinct. Human beings, on the other hand, are not bound by instinct and are given the endless exercise of free will. They must find their own limits to their desires. In this way, we are responsible for the consequences of the exercising of our free will. However, when we look back in history, it is clear that instead of using our free will to make the world a better place, we rained down disaster and confusion on society.

Long ago, between the eleventh and thirteenth century, European countries sent crusades to recapture the holy city of Jerusalem. History revealed that what occurred was an abuse of free will that resulted in needless death and spread confusion throughout the world. Furthermore, the anti-Islamism of the Crusaders and corresponding expansion of Islamic extremism and jihad has continued for seven hundred years to this day and still causes disruption around the world. We also know that the founders of the Americas did not hesitate to slaughter the indigenous natives like animals. Neither intelligence nor reason put a halt to this barbarism. As I mentioned in chapter 2, thought and intelligence are neither objective nor independent. Despite their intelligence, the white people who discovered the Americas did not hesitate to decimate the indigenous natives and saw them as nonhuman because of the differences in their skin color, languages, and cultures.

Humans have chosen modern civilization and urban society as our direction for the future, with the backing of the methodologies of modern science. The modern human race (Homo sapiens) emerged two hundred thousand years ago. At that time, human beings coexisted with the original

Neanderthals. Archaeological findings revealed that they both buried the dead and used flowers for decoration, suggesting early religion. This shows us that from the beginning, humans recognized that even after a person's death, the spirit would survive to either protect or curse the family and its descendants.

The civilized world today essentially depends on thought and intelligence. Human intelligence is elevated to a godly position that is superior to God's There is no need for a God in such a society. From the perspective of modern science, where everything that exists is matter, humans can freely manipulate the laws of science that govern matter and therefore should be able to create everything they need themselves. Indeed, our lives are more convenient and comfortable when we are surrounded by man-made buildings and objects. This is the direction chosen by humankind. The question is, does this choice truly bring us happiness? This reliance on human intelligence is not unprecedented, as examples from the Bible show.

Ancient Civilizations and Religion

The Old Testament in its modern form dates from around the first century. However, some of these writings were actually created in the fifteenth century BC, making them some of the oldest scriptures of humankind. These writings describe myths such as the Tower of Babel and the Great Flood that covered the world when Noah built his ark.

Both these myths first appeared in the Kingdom of Sumer,

located in Mesopotamia more than seven thousand years ago, along with the Gilgamesh epics, which were the oldest known literary works of humankind. These stories had emerged in other countries, and the authors of the Old Testament rewrote them from a monotheistic standpoint. The Sumerians were a mysterious people whose origins are still not fully known. They suddenly appeared in Mesopotamia, in the Middle East, between 7,000 and 9,000 BC and created the oldest urban society in human history with their city-states. At its peak, the population exceeded two hundred thousand people. Said to have believed in polytheism, at their peak, they worshipped as many as five thousand gods.

In the normal view of history, the first religion of humankind was the animism of the barbarians. Monotheism is said to have emerged around 3,500 years ago, when Egypt's Amenhoteb IV worshipped the single god, Aton. However, in her global bestseller, *History of God*, Karen Armstrong counterargues that the Sumerians believed in the one god of the sky. Because this god was so high and far away, it was less accessible to people, and therefore they turned to nature and began to worship its power instead. I agree with Armstrong's theory, but I suspect the Sumerians moved from monotheism to polytheism mainly due to the peculiar characteristics of the human mind, as pointed out later by Bapak. As Sumerian culture developed, their minds started to focus more narrowly on the things of this world, and so naturally, they were less willing to accept a spiritual god from another dimension.

What is remarkable about the Sumerian culture is their Gilgamesh epic, the world's first literary work that has been passed down until today and its story of the flood that covered the world. This historical record of the Sumerians was the first to tell the story of a great flood that would destroy humanity—a legend that has appeared in many parts of the world in the past. The great flood described in the Bible is a modification of the Sumerian story, told from a Judeo-Christian perspective. In it, humans earn the wrath of God through their arrogance and disobedience. God then sends a great flood to destroy humankind. Only Noah and his family, who were faithful to God's will, escaped with the animals in the ark they had built. After drifting in the ocean for a while, they reached a new land and started rebuilding their lives. Interpretation of this story depends on the individual, but it is unlikely that people today would attribute the cause of natural disasters such as floods to God's anger.

Following on from the Sumerians, the Babylonians were also skillful builders and became famous for the Hanging Gardens of Babylon, which were one of the seven wonders of the ancient world. They built cities using brick instead of stone and asphalt instead of plaster. According to the story, at that time, everyone spoke the same language and cooperated with one another. However, they became proud of their technological capabilities and started to build a tower that would reach the heavens, thereby elevating humans to the level of God. The Old Testament says:

They said to each other, "Come, let's make bricks and bake them thoroughly." They used brick instead of stone, and tar for mortar. Then they said, "Come, let us build ourselves a city, with a tower that reaches to the heavens, so that we may make a name for ourselves; otherwise we will be scattered over the face of the whole earth."

But the Lord came down to see the city and the tower the people were building. The Lord said, "If as one people speaking the same language they have begun to do this, then nothing they plan to do will be impossible for them. Come, let us go down and confuse their language so they will not understand each other."

So the Lord scattered them from there over all the earth, and they stopped building the city. That is why it was called Babel—because there the Lord confused the language of the whole world. From there the Lord scattered them over the face of the whole earth.[8]

God's intervention prevented people from cooperating and communicating with one another, and as a result, they were scattered around the world. The Old Testament says this was because God was angry at the behavior of humans.

There are parallels with these stories for modern times; we know now that human actions can bring about natural disasters. Global warming has produced abnormal weather conditions. Recent reports have indicated a rapid decline in insect numbers around the world due to human activity. With an annual decrease of 2.5 percent, in a hundred years, the total number of insects will be 1 percent of what it was before. Some people may think this has little to do with humans, but that is not the case. Without insects, the food chain that supports the earth's ecosystem will collapse, leading to the extinction of all living organisms. Traditionally, we have not given this much thought. In the creation and spread of modern civilization, nobody gave much consideration to the ultimate consequences.

Earth's living organisms have evolved to better adapt to their environment; however, this process took place over eons. The ancestors of our present human race were impatient to have a comfortable and convenient life as soon as possible, and this desire is what ultimately created modern civilization and urban society. Modern civilization does not require God or nature. We have swapped the wilderness for the built environment and rely on tools, equipment, machinery, and other materials. While activities such as *forest bathing*, spending time among mountains and forests, still bring us health benefits, we can now artificially reproduce substances that offer the same health effects as plants. This means people can get the same or better benefits without having to go into the mountains or woods. Is this sufficient for our lives?

The Meaning of Bapak's Cosmic Design

In chapter 2, I explained how thought and intelligence are incapable of true independence and objectivity. In addition, I introduced Bapak's explanation of the structure of the universe and the position of the human within it. I mentioned the higher-order Rohani life force, which is inside our souls and is also our destination after death. During our lifetimes, the knowledge and experience we gain of the worlds below us are what we bring back to the Rohani world. For us, this is more than just a field trip; it is more like an immersed anthropological project where we must inhabit the world to study it.

The life of the human soul does not end there, however, as there are realms in the universe higher than the Rohani level. One of these is the Roh Rachmani force that represents the mercy and love of God. Above this is the Roh Rabanni that represents the creativity of God. Bapak says nothing of these realms that are beyond humans, and we have no way of finding out about them. Even though we are ignorant, it is easy for us to imagine the unfathomable depth and height of the universe and those realms. If this is so, the soul, which has almost infinite life, may be able to travel through the universe toward God. This is because the soul is a part of the universe. Of course, no matter how far you travel, a human being who is finite cannot reach God, who is infinite. It is impossible for us to be one with God—no matter how close we get. God is infinitely further away.

Maybe one day God will erase the universe and recreate it. Then our souls would be nullified, and it would be the very end. The cosmic awareness that Bapak brought to us prompts these thoughts. Using Bapak's cosmology as a map of the entire universe gives us greater perspective of our place within it and provides us with a new understanding. For example, the people who built the Tower of Babel and those who built Noah's ark and survived the Great Flood tried much the same things as modern humans: that is, they attempted to create a society that relies on human thought and intelligence instead of nature, and in doing so became gods. In that sense, civilization today is a modern version of the Tower of Babel. The only difference is that we still do not know the end result of this one.

The negative legacy of our break from reliance on nature's bounties is back pain, near-sightedness, allergies, and other problems bothering many people today; this is probably just the tip of the iceberg. What concerns me more than these physical effects is the impact on our minds and hearts. There is a risk our minds start to become more and more material. Bapak pointed out that human thinking has an affinity with material life forces. That is why we understand the nature of material things and make free use of them. We all know that sometimes a close couple will start to resemble each other in character; sometimes they even start to look like each other because there is so much affinity between them. Little by little, their natures are imprinted on each other. This can happen not only between husband and wife but also between people and things. There already signs that we have become increasingly material; there seem to be more and more heinous crimes, such as indiscriminate murder and child abuse, and people's value is measured in terms of productivity. No doubt, the consequences of these trends will soon be felt by everyone.

Physical or mental stress is usually healed by the natural resilience of the body. If people are not able to cope, continued exposure to even small amounts of stress eventually develops into a physical or mental disease. Most of the time, the person does not realize this until it is too late. I mentioned earlier that people exercise their free will to act more lovingly than an angel or more ruthlessly than the devil. History seems to illustrate that humanity feels more hatred more often than love, and prejudice more often than empathy. People lose their humanity and treat everyone other than their mates as objects.

Scientists still dispute the differences between humans and animals. There are quite a few scientists who think that, while humans developed separately from animals, they are still a species of animal. There is only a small percentage of difference between the genes of wild chimpanzees and modern humans, and this serves to muddy our understanding of these differences. There was a time when it was thought that what differentiated us was our use of tools, but this idea was debunked when more and more cases of animals using tools emerged. If we look to the cosmic origins of human beings as recognized by Bapak, it becomes clear that we are different beings; unlike animal natures, we have morals, and we have a different life purpose. This recognition also overlaps with the Gospel that Jesus brought to humankind. Jesus taught humanity that death was not the end of life and that we should aim for the kingdom of God in heaven as our true destination.

The Grand Design as a Blueprint for the Future

To summarize, I suggest that we use Bapak's cosmology as a kind of grand design for our future. The points below summarize and elaborate on the reasons for this, which I have dealt with so far.

1. First, there is our sense of incongruity with this world.

    As I mentioned, many people have a vague sense of incongruity about their place in the world. This is because this world is not the home of the human soul. Bapak talked about the time when Adam was sent to Earth from heaven. He said that Adam wept because he did not want to be sent to the material world. However, the more he lived in this world and grew familiar with life here, the more attached to the world he became. When the time came to die, he pleaded with God for a longer life.

2. Why are human beings pulled in two directions, from above and below?

While human beings have a desire to improve and push themselves beyond their limits, they are constantly tempted by the thoughts and emotions of the forces below them. We can understand this dilemma in the light of Bapak's cosmic structure as a grand design. The human world is suspended in the middle of this cosmic structure, between the higher world above and the lower worlds below.

3. Bapak's explanations on death.

The three questions Gaugin wrote on the back of his famous canvas can be answered by Bapak's understanding of the universe and our place within it. When we are born, our soul comes from the Rohani world, which also forms its content. Our special role is to carry the experience and knowledge gained in this world back to the Rohani world after we die. Our destination after death is not the material world, therefore, but the Rohani world. Bapak's other comments on death are short but meaningful. For example, he mentioned that everything that exists in this world also exists in the next; only its manner of existence is different. This allows us to conjecture the relationship and differences between this world and the next.

4. Bapak's views on scientific materialism as the cause for the materialistic beliefs of people today.

Materialism was one of many philosophical theories in ancient Greece. In the seventeenth century, modern science emerged as a new way to view the world, which was different from philosophy and religion. This spread around the world under the guise of scientific materialism, with outcomes such as Marx's dialectic materialism and communism.

Where once religion could enlighten people in the areas that science cannot reach, such as the fate and state of a soul after death, the religious people themselves have turned, even doubting in the existence of an afterlife. Religion is becoming a mere shell as a result. Religious leaders are attempting to stem religion's decline, but they do not know how. We are facing that reality in a globalized world. We live with the anxiety and loneliness that arise from this, and there seems no way out. For a while at least, it seems we can only watch events unfold.

Humanity has encountered crisis situations many times in the past and has overcome them. We can only hope that humanity will overcome the current plague of anxiety and loneliness and create a bright future. However, to allow this to happen, we must change our current obsession with fulfilling desire and instead aim for a more cooperative society. The worldview and morality required for this to happen have not been agreed upon; indeed, the discussion has barely begun.

Artificial intelligence (AI) has developed rapidly and has already exceeded many of the capabilities of the human brain. However, AI cannot develop human character, and there is greater risk of people becoming more and more obsessed with the material as our civilization keeps growing. If we allow Bapak's understanding of the universe and our place within it to underpin everything, our perspective will expand, and the significance and purpose of human beings will be become visible on a cosmic scale. We will be able to see that this material world is only a temporary dwelling for human beings.

It may be that I have simply opened Pandora's box. In the story, Pandora's box hid a small child named Hope. As an author, I would like this to be true. At the very least, I hope this book will have the effect of broadening your horizons.

I wish you the best and a fruitful life.

EPILOGUE

MODERN SOCIETY AND THE THREAT OF COVID-19

This book was completed more than a year and half before the emergence of the novel coronavirus in China, and there is, therefore, no mention of the virus within the book, nor do the contents represent a response to it.

The book was prompted by the unexpectedly rapid progress of globalization, thanks to the revolution in digital communications and IT, and was written with a specific goal in mind. That goal was to seek to analyze the characteristics of this new society and what it means for us humans who live in it. I wanted to explore how much we know about ourselves and how much or how little we understand about the earth we live on.

As I mention in the book, science underpins today's world. The birth of modern science began with a battle that took place in a medieval courtroom between absolutist Christian theologians and new scientists represented by Galileo Galilei. This was really a battle for hegemony with links to international politics. The outcome was a growing separation between the two, where theologians mistook science as their enemy since it denies the existence of God and religion, and scientists mistook religion as their enemy since it denies the existence of objective facts.

On the one hand, science continues to progress; long-established views are replaced by new theories, and this cycle will continue. On the other hand, religion governs a large part of life that cannot be ruled by scientific rationalism, such as God, belief, and the soul. It provides meaning to people's lives.

For this reason, I believe that modern science was established with a fatal flaw: the decision to dismiss any phenomena that could not be scientifically observed and quantified. Our lives are colored by a myriad of beliefs and perceptions, including God and the soul, and to eliminate these is to greatly narrow down the human experience and understanding.

We are inundated with scientific knowledge and discoveries, but we have lost an understanding of where we fit in the overall picture and what direction we should head in next. We are the traveler who sees only the rocks and trees and not the forest, or the fisherman who knows the fish and seabirds but not where he is in the vast ocean at this moment.

This book also mentions the strange phenomenon of elementary particles and introduces quantum theory. We looked at how, astonishingly, these particles seem to have two opposing properties whereby at one and the same time they can be particles (solids) and waves (vibrations). Furthermore, these properties change from one to the other, depending on whether they are being observed or not. For example, the moment we try to discover the position and movement vector of an elementary particle, it appears to switch from being a wave form to a solid form.

Science cannot fully explain why the properties of these particles change when there is human interaction. Mohammad Subuh, the founder of the Subud movement, did say something that could explain this. He mentioned that humans are specialized in understanding the things of this world, but we were not given the ability to perceive spiritual vibrations such as waveforms. For example, even the waveforms of light and sound are out of reach to us once they exceed a certain range. Mohammad Subuh went on to say that we will never be able to understand the truth of the spiritual world, and no matter how hard we try, our conclusions will always be misguided.

Science is the mainstay of all modern civilization. Countless machines and devices have been invented to make our lives easier, and we live in increasingly urban areas as civilization hastens its spread around the globe. My concern is that this process has brought with it the undeniable side effect of a creeping materialism of human life. This is manifest as a tendency to place others on a par with objects and view them as material things. I would be relieved if the thought that this trend is growing is mine alone. If it is indeed what characterizes the new societies of the age, what kind of future can humanity expect?

Despite concerted efforts around the world, the COVID-19

virus infection still has the potential to infect everyone. Our biggest concern right now is how soon we can end this pandemic, and there is no definitive answer to this. People are anxious, and tensions are high. With this continuing situation, the potential for riots to occur in poorer regions and for these to spread further cannot be ruled out.

It is not my intention to elaborate on this topic here, as we have reached the end of my book. My greatest hope is that, despite its faults, this book can prompt readers to reassess what they take for granted and perhaps gain new perspectives on their lives.

COPYRIGHT

REFERENCES

9 M. S. Sumohadiwidjojo, *Autobiography* (UK: Subud Publications International Ltd., 1990), 29.

10 Sumohadiwidjojo, *Autobiography*, 29.

11 Naoki Kashio, *Supirichuariti kakumei: Gendai resiseibunka to shukyo no kanosei* (*Spirituality Revolution: Contemporary Spiritual Culture and the Possibility of Open Religiosity*) (Tokyo: Shunjusha, 2010).

12 Fumiaki Miyamoto, *Oboe to no jikan (toki)*. (Tokyo: Jiji Press, 2007)

Printed in the United States
By Bookmasters